From Jamestown
To Jamestown

Letters to an African Child
Kojo Yankah

"Until lions have their historians, tales of hunting will always glorify the hunter." (African Proverb)

Habari Afrika !

Dedication

This book is dedicated to all children of African descent who are striving to rediscover themselves and build a proud identity for themselves.

Books by Kojo Yankah

1. From Jamestown to Jamestown (2019)
2. The Trial of JJ Rawlings (revised 2018)
3. Our Motherland-My Life (2017)
4. Proactive Public Relations (2011) with Chris Skinner
5. Otumfuo Osei Tutu Il - the King on the Golden Stool(2010)
6. Introduction to Branding & Marketing Communication
    Management (Ed. 2007)
7. The Story of Namibia (1990)
8. Dialogue with the North (1990)
9. The Last Journey (1989)
10. Crossroads at Ankobea (1982)

Lest We Forget

The regeneration of Africa means that a new and unique civilization is soon to be added to the world. The African is not a proletarian in the world of science and art: he has precious creations of his own—of ivory; of copper and of gold; of fine, plaited willow-ware; and weapons of superior workmanship.

Civilization resembles an organic being in its development—it is born, it perishes, and it can propagate itself. The most essential departure of this new civilization is that it shall be thoroughly spiritual and humanistic-indeed, a regeneration moral and eternal. - **Isaka Seme***, (South African)*

"The Regeneration of Africa", in *The Journal of the Royal African Society,* Vol.5 (1905-1906)

Freedom is not a commodity which is given to the 'enslaved' upon demand. It is a precious reward, the shining trophy of struggle and sacrifice. - **Kwame Nkrumah** (Ghana)

Introduction to Africa Must Unite, 1963

Acknowledgements

To the many researchers, historians, novelists, writers, museums and educators of African descent, too many to list, whose works helped open my eyes to the untold truths behind the African identity, struggles and freedom;

To Halif Khalif Khalifah, publisher, for inviting me in 1994 to attend the 375th anniversary of the first African to land in America held in Jamestown, near Hampton, Virginia, which nurtured this project;

To Drs Efua and Esi Sutherland, Mr Akunu Dake, Rabbi Kohain Halevi, Prof James Small, and Dr Lionel Jeffries for deep insights we have shared together since we joined the PANAFEST Movement;

To Dr Joseph Silver & Dr Carlton Brown of Savannah and Atlanta and their beautiful families for opening their doors and hearts to share in a true African familyhood;

Professor Kofi Asare Opoku, my spiritual senior brother; custodian of African wisdom;

To my wife, Nana Nyarkoa, who has always provided administrative and moral support; and

To all my wonderful children and grandchildren who while admiring my 'energy level' have always boosted me up with their comments, encouragement and pride.

Previews

    Young people of all races are mostly oblivious to the reality of the struggles of "African people" historically and contemporarily. They do not know because there has been a conscious effort to eliminate this history; and, they have been deceived in such a way to suggest that "it" [the history] never existed. Mr. Yankah, in his book, **From Jamestown to Jamestown: Letters to an African Child,** has chronicled the true history of Africa and the Diaspora during a critical period in a manner that will gain the attention of folk across races, across continents, and across generations. His unique approach to sharing history though letters is sure to create a readership that is more informed about the history of African people throughout the Diaspora. This is a "must read" book which traces the African people from Jamestown, Africa to Jamestown, Virginia highlighting their journey and their challenges along the way.

    In telling this history, Kojo Yankah links the great African luminaries and leaders and the African American luminaries and leaders and their writings to the Bible and other mainstream literature. In doing so, he points out the truth and the contradictions when the various sources are juxtaposed to each other. Only when the truth is told, as is done in this book, will people realize that the first British and the first Chinese were of African descent. The DNA does not lie! What else has been hidden from the world? Read the book and find out! Remember as one writer stated: "A half truth is a whole lie." Going forward, the world needs the "whole truth." **From Jamestown to Jamestown: Letters to an African Child,** is an attempt to inspire further inquiry into critical matters that have been shaped by the perspectives of people other than Africans and those in the Diaspora.

Joseph H. Silver, Ph.D, Atlanta, USA

From Jamestown to Jamestown-Letters to an African Child, is a thoughtfully refreshing account of African history that pensively reflects the ancestral wisdom of our African forebears that urges lions to tell their own stories instead of relying on stories that hunters always tell to glorify themselves, at the ruinous expense of lions. In a word, Efo Kojo tells the lions' tale of African history to a young African (and to older ones as well), Ayesha - she who lives; and it is only when Africans can tell their own stories from their perspective that they can amply safeguard their ever-abiding consciousness and substantial identity.

Centuries of other peoples' narration of African history has beclouded the truth about Africans and their history, and in this case the truth about Africans and their history may be said to have become skinny, but the Kenyan proverb stoutly affirms, "The truth may become skinny, but will never perish!" And the truth that was seemingly lost in the morning has started to come home in the evening in **From Jamestown to Jamestown**, which tells the story of Africa as the cradle of humans and human civilization, through the various epochs in African history to the present and demonstrating clearly that our truth is undeniably different from the opinions of others.

The admirably skillful way in which the author manages to tell the story in the form of letters, manageable doses of life-sustaining historical information, and all in language that is not perceptively intimidating, should appeal, especially, to Ayesha and her generation. And the value of the information contained in the book may be found in the question, "what would become of our children if they possessed the information contained in this book?" This is a must reading for Ayesha and her contemporaries as well as their parents and grandparents.

Kofi Asare Opoku, Professor, Africana Studies

From Jamestown to Jamestown! This book is a must-read! Wow! It was simply insightful and thought-provoking. It makes history so easy to read and conceptualize.

As I read, I kept imagining Ayesha, a fifteen-year old sitting in the library, her eyes hungry for the immense knowledge in this phenomenal book. History had never come alive to her in this way. She is questioning all the things she learnt in her social studies class about the Trans-Atlantic Slave Trade, about the origins of civilization and she begins to see herself as a powerful force to reckon with. She is angry at the inhumane treatment meted out to her ancestors like that of Olaudah. Her understanding of religion and Christianity is challenged as she struggles to reconcile how the Bible was once used to justify slavery and even the apartheid in South Africa. She also reads about slaves in the Southern part of America and the insurrection led by educated minister and slave Nat Turner to free every black man, woman and child from chattel slavery and every form of oppression. She has a better understanding of what the Civil War is all about and terms like Jim Crow make more sense to her. She now fully understands the essence of becoming allies with her African counterparts in the diaspora.

The eyes of her understanding have been enlightened and after reading this powerful history, she vows to read more about her African identity and to work with Africans in the diaspora to rebuild the Africa we need. She runs home to share this revelation with everyone she knows. Marcus Garvey's words remind her that "The Black skin is not a badge of shame, but rather a glorious symbol of national greatness." After reading *From Jamestown to Jamestown*, she is poised with a new sense of identity and armed with knowledge to liberate not just herself but her community and her nation.

Maame Nyarkoa Yankah, (University Student), USA

Having personally been informed and armed to rethink my *Africanness* and how to foster intercontinental relations with other people of African descent in the diaspora, I unreservedly recommend the, '**From Jamestown to Jamestown - *Letters to an African Child*** to historians, anthropologists, linguists, scholars of religions, seekers of sublime truth, and pupils and students. They will all have an uncommon taste of African culture, history, language, and religion from the book. More importantly, they will be armed to help liberate the continent of Africa from its poly-challenges!

Charles Prempeh, Ph.D. Candidate, University of Cambridge, U.K.

Lift Every Voice and Sing
(James Weldon Johnson – 1871-1938)

Lift every voice and sing,
Till earth and heaven ring,
Ring with the harmonies of Liberty;
Let our rejoicing rise
High as the list'ning skies,
Let it resound loud as the rolling sea.
Sing a song full of the faith that the dark past has taught us,
Sing a song full of the hope that the present has brought us;
Facing the rising sun of our new day begun,
Let us march on till victory is won.

Stony the road we trod,
Bitter the chast'ning rod,
Felt in the days when hope unborn had died;
Yet with a steady beat,
Have not our weary feet
Come to the place for which our fathers sighed?
We have come over a way that with tears has been watered.
We have come, treading our path through the blood of the
slaughtered,
Out from the gloomy past,
Till now we stand at last
Where the white gleam of our bright star is cast.

Contents

Foreword

by Dr Arikana Chihombori-Quao

The story of the African will continue to be told. There is ample literature on the field claiming to be stories about the continent or the people of Africa. Yet, we know that until recently, most writings painted a continent without history and without any civilization. Then, others separated Africa from the Diaspora.

There is also the case of peoples of African descent and on the continent being miseducated about themselves, giving room for them to misunderstand themselves, and sometimes violently denigrating themselves.

Yet, the source of all civilization is now known to be the River Nile in Africa out of which researchers are now agreeing to be the origin of man and the black color.

Why this book by Kojo Yankah has come at the right time is that he backs his 'Letters to an African Child' with well-researched materials from the continent and the diaspora to provide a united voice to the call for a United States of Africa. African scholars like Cheikh Anta Diop and Ibn Batuta from the continent, listed alongside African American historians and academics like WEB Du Bois, Carter Woodson up till Henry Louis Gates and Molefi Kete Asante, clarify the African civilization so eloquently. But the beauty of Kojo Yankah's style of writing is that he breaks down Africa's story into very simple language that can be easily understood by the fifteen year old Ayesha as well as her parents and grandparents.

Starting casually from a pub in Jamestown, Accra, which used to have a slave fort, the narrator takes his readers through a historical journey from the inception of the ignominious slave trade, through the inhuman treatment of captives in dungeons and across the Atlantic Ocean to the Americas. He captures brilliantly several incidents of resistance put up by the captives till the major rebellions that occurred in the Caribbean and the Southern States of America, leading to the American Civil War.

Kojo Yankah treats the subject of the European Scramble for Africa as the boiling point from which Africans ignited the movement for self-determination. The thread that links the struggle of blacks for Civil Rights to the fight for freedom on the continent is masterfully crafted by the writer to make the joint agitation for racial equality, freedom and justice complete. Various gatherings of African liberation fighters, trade unionists, and political activists were climaxed at the Manchester Conference of 1945 from where new strategies were designed to take Africa forward.

What happened in the Caribbean, and on mainland America, leading to the American Civil War is captured in these 'Letters to an African Child'. And so is the Civil Rights Movement which saw America through its Jim Crow laws and the violence that it unleashed on both sides. In Africa, it fell on the leaders, like Kwame Nkrumah and Jomo Kenyatta, who studied in America and England to go back to the continent to liberate their people from colonial rule.

So, you have captives being taken out of Jamestown, Africa having endured all the indignities from their European captors to settle in Jamestown, Virginia, fighting back for Racial Equality.

What a story!

Today, Africa is faced with the gigantic task of uniting its natural and human resources to build a world power to make its citizens and those in the diaspora proud of their achievements and their civilization. There could not be a better time for Kojo Yankah to add this major contribution to the efforts to re-educate the world about the potential of the African to surmount all difficulties despite the horrible treatment meted out to the continent and its peoples.

I can see this book filling the gap that miseducation has created for Africans on the continent as well as in the diaspora. It is a book to read in every home, school and library.

If you enjoy reading this book, which I am sure you will, what will strike you is the uncommon literary style the author uses to tell the story of emancipation. It is a masterpiece.

HE Arikana Chihombori-Quao, M.D.
Ambassador, African Union, Washington DC
June 12, 2019

Preface

by **Ladi Nylander,** Jamestown, Accra, Ghana

This book is about the experience of black emancipation. It follows the journey through the centuries of the unique "African Personality". The book is being published on the 400th anniversary of the arrival of the first black slaves into Jamestown, Virginia, USA. This gives us cause to explore the many coincidences that pull the African diaspora closer to Africa; and to examine the indomitable spirit of the black race. Despite the many vicissitudes that afflicted the experience, the black race managed to preserve its relative homogeneity and sense of kinship. This is remarkable in view of the countless incidents that occurred during this journey to potentially fracture this uniqueness

Jamestown, Accra, Ghana was established over sixty years after Jamestown, Virginia, USA. One cannot help but imagine how the destinies of these two cities would converge at numerous points along the journey. This book is an exploration and celebration of those many moments. The chapters clearly reflect the mutual interdependence of people of African descent around the world.

Jamestown, Virginia, USA came into being when three British ships ("Susan Constant", "Godspeed" and "Discovery") with one hundred able-bodied men sailed into Chesapeake Bay in 1607 and entered into the 'New World'. They had been sent by the London Company to search for treasure; to evangelize the Christian faith among the native population; and to raise crops that England could not grow at home. Sailing into the interior they settled near a river which they named James River after their monarch, King James I. They also founded a settlement near the James River which they named Jamestown.

The Gold Coast (now Ghana) occupied a modest parcel of land on the West African coast. It was however immensely wealthy in the goods then in popular demand in European markets. It attracted ships and traders from practically every seafaring nation in Western Europe. These included the Portuguese, the French, the Danes, the British and the Brandenburgers. The sixteenth to the nineteenth century were the high points of the slave trade. It was a period of great insecurity for all the communities involved. Over fifty-four European forts and castles were erected on the shores of the Gold Coast to protect European trade, their staff and themselves.

This period must have been one of the lowest points of the world's and indeed of human history. Accra was one of the principal market towns along the coast. Three of these European forts were located on its Atlantic shore. The first one was the Dutch fort of Crevecouer built in 1641. The second was the Swedish/Danish fort of Christianborg erected in 1659. The third and final one was Fort St James built by the English in 1673 under a Royal Charter from King James II of Great Britain.

The Gold Coast had the reputation in the seventeenth and eighteenth century as the white mans' grave. This was because of the high incidence of tropical diseases with no known cures. Few Europeans survived long enough in the tropics to help build the forts. The English were lucky to find a highly experienced workforce of local artisans familiar with medieval European construction gained from the two earlier European forts.

They therefore built James Fort largely with African artisans and laborers. Workers were recruited from towns along the coast including present day Elmina, Cape Coast and Prampram. Many were imported from the surrounding regions especially from the town of Allada in present day Nigeria. So many Yorubas were brought in that, today, Ghanaians identify Yorubas as Alata people. They became a significant population of Jamestown which became known as Ngleshie (English) Alata. Jamestown, Accra was founded at the height of the slave trade.

It is not by any means far-fetched to conjecture therefore that elements that often connected Jamestown, Virgina and Jamestown, Accra were very much at play in various forms. The security of the inhabitants in Jamestown, Accra, was of principal concern to its founders.

Consequently, Jamestown had a huge diversity of residents who communicated in mutually incomprehensible languages. The language with the widest currency was a vehicular pidgin Portuguese invented at the end of the fifteenth century. This had developed when Portuguese traders were the first Europeans to arrive on the coast to trade. This pidgin Portuguese has largely disappeared in the local parlance; and it has been replaced equally by a pidgin English variety.

Traces of the earlier pidgin can still be heard in occasional words and phrases in the language of present-day Jamestown, Accra. Jamestown, Accra prospered as a trading center and, its unique association with the English, helped the town to survive the end of the slave trade. It recovered as the main export center for the Gold Coast when palm oil and rubber emerged as the principal exports from the Gold Coast during the last decade of the nineteenth century. Eventually these two commodities were important to fuel the rising industrial experience in Europe.

Meanwhile the slave trade had continued its ignominious course. It was, to use the words of one historian in the 1890s, "an unmitigated misery - a crime unredeemed by one extenuating circumstance."

This book charters that horrible experience.

Since the 1960's many African countries have demonstrated that their structural weaknesses inherent in their initial formations make them easy pawns in the hands of their former colonial masters. This is a major detriment to Africa's progress. The seeds sewn by that inglorious slave trade experience remain to plague Africa and, even today, the "plundering" continues.

African leaders need more than ever to work together within the overall objectives of the African Union. At the dawn of independence, Kwame Nkrumah of Ghana had remarked that "the independence of Ghana is meaningless, unless it is linked-up with the total liberation of the African Continent". Have those memorable words now finally "come home to roost"? The experiences of "**Jamestown to Jamestown-Letters to an African Child**" seek to answer that question.

Ladi Nylander
Jamestown, Accra
May 2019

Jamestown Port, Jamestown, Accra Ghana

Chapter 1

AYESHA

"If we are going to be masters of our destiny, we must be masters of the ideas that influence that destiny" – John Henrik Clarke (1915-1998)

My dear Ayesha,

I am writing you these letters because you represent millions of youth in the world who have a little blood of the African in you. You may be living anywhere on this earth. Some of your older brothers and sisters are struggling to make a career for themselves. Others cannot understand why, in spite of all their efforts, they cannot reach their goals and aspirations. Some are languishing in jail. Others are making a living for themselves because they followed a certain path prescribed by their parents, relations or just guardians. Others didn't have any roadmaps, either because they didn't have any, or else they abandoned the ones shown them. Yet, others are described or labeled as stars or celebrities because they shone in the classroom, on the sports field or on the stage.

Dear Ayesha,

Some of your peers inspire you because they took some decisions, some very risky ones, to get to where they are. They took initiatives, dared themselves and everybody else and made life better for themselves. And what does it mean by making life better for oneself? Is it the location where you find yourself; is it the car, the house, or the vacations you enjoy? Or is it your ability to donate to charities and make a difference in other people's lives?

Yet, others cannot make ends meet. They have given up hope of rising because somebody has told them they belong to an inferior class and they should be satisfied where they are in life. They have been cowed down with fear from fellow human beings. They have been shown images of the black being always subservient. They have been told to forget about their own history because it does not give them any hope or pride.

Dear Ayesha,

You most likely do not know why you find yourself in the geographical location where you are – in South America, in the Caribbean, in Asia, in Africa, in North America, or in Europe - speaking a different language from another person of similar color as yours; having a different temperament and a unique outlook on life. You meet a person of the same color as yours and you realize you have different religions and different faiths. You sometimes greet or do not greet each other because of the orientation or the intuition you have about each other. Otherwise, some kind of education you have received through your parentage, through the classroom, or even through the media, has turned you in the direction of one another or else turned you off and made you suspect or hate each other.

Dear Ayesha,

I am writing to you because your name resonates in several parts of the world. As soon as you mention your name, they ask you where you come from. Some may even wonder why you are so bold. Tell them you are created by a Supreme Being to be part of this great universe. You represent the youth who do not even know that the black in you defines you as the mother of all inventions, the mother of science and technology, the mother of the arts; you are the mother of world civilization. You are my African Child.

Dear Ayesha,

This book is inspired by the vision that one day, Africans, on the continent and in the diaspora, will be reunited in a United States of Africa. The struggle and the journey will be long and arduous, but they will be fuelled by the true history, common culture, resilient spirit and the sheer optimism of the people.

The Anthem of the African Union says in part:

Let us all unite and celebrate together
The victories won for our liberation.
Let us dedicate ourselves to rise together
To defend our liberty and unity
O Sons and Daughters of Africa
Flesh of the Sun and Flesh of the Sky
Let us make Africa the Tree of Life.

Dear Ayesha,

The February7th,2018 edition of 'The Guardian' of London published an article that may have escaped a lot of Africans. Science correspondent, Hannah Devlin, revealed a new scientific finding that states, and confirms, that 'the first modern Britons, who lived about 10,000 years ago, had 'dark to black skin'.

The story says this comes from a ground-breaking DNA analysis of Britain's oldest complete skeleton. The article says that 'it was initially assumed that Cheddar Man, the fossil, had pale skin and fair hair, but his DNA paints a different picture, strongly suggesting he had blue eyes, a very dark to black complexion and dark curly hair'.

Dear Ayesha,

Prior to this, on November 6, 1999, Professor Jin Li of Fudan University, Shangai, published that modern humans evolved from a single origin, and that Chinese people originated from East Africa some 100, 000 years ago. In his work, Book on the glory of Blacks over Whites, cited by Lisapo Ya Kama, Al-Jahiz, a black multidisciplinary scholar from Iraq writing in Arabic language, states: "The Ethiopians, the Berbers, the Copts, the Nubians, the Zaghawa, the Moors, the people of Sindh, the Hindus, the Qamar, the Daliba, the Chinese, and those of beyond…the islands of the Seas,,,teem with blacks, up to the Hindustan and China". The work of Al-Jahiz (776-869 is what has been confirmed by Chinese archaeologists. The skull of Qafzeh, the oldest modern man of Asia, dates back 100,000 years, found in the American Museum of Natural History, and 'the anatomically modern man was born in Africa 200,000 years ago in the Great Lakes Region'.

Scientists Nicholas Crawford, Derek Kelly, Matthew Hansen and Mercia Beltram have published in **Science** magazine, Volume 358, Issue 6365, November 2017 a study that traces the evolution of genes and how they traveled around the world.'While the dark skin of some Pacific Islanders can be traced to Africa, gene variants from Eurasia also seem to have made their way back to Africa. And surprisingly, some of the mutations responsible for lighter skin in Europeans turn out to have an ancient African origin'. Geneticist Greg Barsh of the Hudson Alpha Institute of Biotechnology describes the study as 'a really a landmark study of skin color diversity'.

Is this very important?

My dear Ayesha,

Yes, it is. Today, thanks to enormous research in Archaeology, Anthropology, History, Science & Technology, and of course the world-wide-web, we know for certain that original world civilization began in Africa. We now know that it was all a lie when we were taught for hundreds of years that Africans had no history, and that Christopher Columbus 'discovered' Africa.

We now know from books and researched material from scholars like John Henrik Clarke, Cheikh Anta Diop, WEB Du Bois, Basil Davidson, Ibn Battuta, LSB Leakey, Robin Walker, Chancellor Williams, Lerone Bennett,Jr, Edward Baptist, George GM James, Molefi Kete Asante, Louis Gates and many more, that for many hundreds of centuries, Africa was in the forefront of all world progress, and that we have been fed with lies that have always kept black people as an inferior race. I am convinced that Africans once ruled the world, and that the story of the African has been distorted. And I know that the process to decolonise our minds has begun.

It is now known that the origins of European culture trace their roots to the ancient African civilizations of the Nile Valley, and that there were deliberate efforts to destroy and hide traces of African heritage.

Dear Ayesha,

Fast forward to the 16th and 17th century, ship loads of Africans were taken out of south-western Africa to Mexico, Brazil, North, Central and South Americas, and the Caribbean.

About the middle of 1800, the official Scramble for Africa began in earnest, and Africa was divided and shared like pieces of cake to European powers that needed to industrialize their economies.

In the 20th century, forces of resistance got to a height from various parts of the world to culminate in the many boycotts, wars, meetings, conferences and demonstrations that centred on the liberation of the black man from the bonds of subjugation, oppression and repression, and the restoration of the dignity and freedom of not only the African continent but of blacks everywhere in the world.

Dear Ayesha,

The statement of eminent black scholar WEB Du Bois, at the 1945 Manchester Conference, rings loud today:

"When once the blacks of the US, the West Indies and Africa work and think together, the future of the black man in the modern world is safe".

It is estimated that blacks in the diaspora constitute about 140million people.

Available statistics (2018) show that Brazil has 56million blacks, United States 47million, Haiti 9million, Dominican Republic 8million, Colombia 5million, France 4million, Venezuela 3.5million, Jamaica 3million., United Kingdom 2.5million, Mexico 1.5million, Peru 1.3million, Canada 1.2million, Cuba 1.2million, Italy 1.2million, Puerto Rico 1million, Germany 900,000, Ecuador 700,000, Spain 700,000, Trinidad & Tobago 500,000, Barbados 250,000, Guyana 240,000, Suriname 200,000, Argentina 150,000, Grenada 100,000.

Add to these numbers (140m) the population of the African Union estimated at 1.2 billion. This is the United States of Africa we are talking about. Compare with China's 1.4billion, India's 1.2billion, Russia's 144million, European Union's 514million, and USA's 312million.

The African Union defines the African diaspora as consisting of 'people of African origin living outside the continent, irrespective of their citizenship and nationality and who are willing to work for the development of the continent and the building of the African Union'.

Dear Ayesha,

In Ghana before 1957, school children, like me, saluted the Union Jack, the official flag of the United Kingdom. We recited the words that went with the national anthem "God Save The Queen".

The words:

"God save our gracious Queen
Long live our noble Queen
God save the Queen
Send her victorious, Happy and glorious,
Long to reign over us
God save the Queen".

Dear Ayesha,

On March 6,1957, under the leadership of Osagyefo Kwame Nkrumah, Ghana gained independence, the Ghana Flag replaced the Union Jack, and a new National Anthem replaced 'God Save the Queen':

"Lift High the Flag of Ghana".

In the words of the Ghana National Anthem now,
The first verse says :

"God bless our Homeland Ghana
And make our nation great and strong,
Bold to defend forever
The cause of Freedom and of Right.
Fill our hearts with true humility
Make us cherish fearless honesty,
And help us to resist oppressors' rule
With all our will and might for evermore".

Significantly, the first two lines of the 3rd stanza are sometimes lost:

"Raise high the flag of Ghana
*And **one with Africa** advance".*

Ghana is compelled by her historical circumstances, foundation, and standing in African affairs to advance her fortunes alongside the rest of Africa and the diaspora.

Kwame Nkrumah left Ghanaians with the indelible admonition:

"The Independence of Ghana is meaningless unless it is linked up with the total liberation of the African continent".

Divided we are weak; united, Africa could become one of the greatest forces for good in the world.' – Kwame Nkrumah.

Dear Ayesha,

Before, and long after independence was declared, children in Ghana, like in all British colonies, studied British and European civilization in schools. We knew more about the British Isles, Europe and North America than we did about Africa.

African ancestral beliefs were equated with the devil, and new European values were taught to those who could qualify to go to school. Significantly all the books we studied were written to a large extent by white historians.

What was the image of Africans in the Diaspora like?

Before Kwame Nkrumah, we were never taught to see blacks in the diaspora as kith and kin. Never.

The period of street agitations for civil and equal rights in other parts of the world was portrayed to Africans on television as a representation of black, lazy and unproductive folks who wanted to bring down the stable economic and democratic society of America.

Dear Ayesha,

We, students, never learnt anything about the inhuman and horrible treatment meted out to Africans who were taken across the seas through what has come to be called the Trans-Atlantic Slave Trade. Never did we learn anything positive about the black resistance movement and contributions of Americans of African descent during the period of the making of the United States of America.

My dear Ayesha,

For a few of us who were politically alert because of our pan-Africanist orientation through the Young Pioneer Movement in Ghana, we went a step further. At the University of Ghana, where

Kwame Nkrumah had opened the Institute of African Studies, we found the admission of a number of African American and diaspora students as an opportunity to be more curious.

In the late 1960s and early 70s, my Ghanaian colleagues and some black friends decided to form the International Black Alliance. Our objective was: To bridge the gap between the two sides. We wanted a better understanding of each other.

We mounted Public Lectures, Symposia, Seminars and held monthly meetings to give opportunity to individuals to share experiences and ideas. This was most productive, and our numbers shot up over time.

We read books and writings by Carter Woodson, WEB Du Bois, Marcus Garvey, Malcolm X, Stokely Carmichael (Kwame Toure) and poetry of black writers like James Baldwin and Maya Angelou. We followed stories of black leaders in the civil rights movement and shared information from across university campuses worldwide. We educated ourselves about progressive African leaders like Azikiwe, Nyerere, Kenyatta, Lumumba, Sekou Toure and others.

Dear Ayesha,

When I had the opportunity to teach at my former high school Adisadel College, in Cape Coast, Ghana, in the early 70s, I launched the Pan African Forum, and registered quite a number of students for the study of Pan-African affairs including the Black Liberation Movements in various parts of the world.

I am aware that the miseducation continued in many other schools.

Dear Ayesha,

From the interaction I had, I learnt that the miseducation I am talking about was even worse in the Diaspora.

Carter Godwin Woodson summarises the situation in America in his book entitled '**The Mis-education of the Negro**':

"The philosophy and ethics resulting from our educational system have justified slavery, peonage, segregation and lynching.'

"The 'educated Negroes' have the attitude of contempt toward their own people as well as in their mixed schools; **Negroes are taught to admire the Hebrew, the Greek, the Latin and the Teuton and to despise the African**".

On both sides of the Atlantic, the thought of inferiority of the black man was drilled in the minds of students in every class or community.

And, of course, when you control a man's thinking you do not have to worry about his actions.

Dear Ayesha,

It is happening in our everyday lives even today. The situation has not changed much.

Throughout my experience and life as a student of Pan-Africanism, one truth has always come to confront me: Africans on the continent, as well as Africans in the diaspora are equally mis-educated, first about themselves, and second about each other. And that until a conscious effort is made on both sides to educate ourselves, our unity will be seriously undermined.

Dear Ayesha,

The Pan African Historical Theatre Festival (PANAFEST) was first launched in Ghana in 1992; two years later, l was offered the chair of the Publicity Committee and l toured, together with other officials, the United Kingdom, North America, Brazil and the Caribbean countries, in addition to various parts of Africa, to promote the need for all of us to join hands in 'Uniting the African Family'. Much later, in 1999, l was elected chairman of PANAFEST for another 10 years, to institutionalize the mission to unite the African family and give a rebirth to African Civilization.

The third verse of the Black National Anthem which we sang at PANAFEST says:

God of our weary years,
God of our silent tears,
Thou who hast brought us thus far on the way;
Thou who hast by Thy might,
Led us into the light,
Keep us forever in the path, we pray.
Lest our feet stray from the places, our God, where we met Thee,
Lest our hearts, drunk with the wine of the world, we forget Thee;
Shadowed beneath Thy hand,
May we forever stand,
True to our God,
True to our native land.

Dear Ayesha, this song was composed sometime in 1899, by a young poet and school principal named James Weldon Johnson. He was asked to address a crowd in Jacksonville, Florida, for the coming anniversary of Abraham Lincoln's birthday.

Instead of preparing a speech, Johnson decided to write a poem. He used the opportunity of paying tribute to Abraham Lincoln for his role in the abolition of slavery to wake up African Americans with a call to action: **"Lift ev'ry voice and sing."**

After finishing each stanza, he handed over the lyrics to his classically trained brother, John Rosamond Johnson, who put the words to music. I remember my attorney friend from California, William Agbeko Davis, who introduced the cd for the song for the first time at PANAFEST/Emancipation Day in Ghana.

Dear Ayesha,
Listen to our brothers and sisters from the four corners of the African continent.

From South Africa, their anthem composed originally in their native language by a Methodist school teacher named Enoch Sontonga in 1897, now sang in five local languages:

Nkosi sikelel' iAfrika

God (Lord) bless Africa
May her glory be lifted high
Hear our petitions
God bless us

Your children
God we ask you to protect our nation
Intervene and end all conflicts
Protect us
Protect our nation
Our nation, South Africa
South Africa...

Ringing out from our blue heavens
From our deep seas breaking round
Over everlasting mountains
Where the echoing crags resound

Sounds the call to come together,
And united we shall stand,
Let us live and strive for freedom,
In South Africa our land.

From Kenya comes their anthem originally composed and sang in Kiswahili:

Ee Mungu nguvu yetu

O God of all creation
Bless this our land and nation

Justice be our shield and defender
May we dwell in unity Peace and liberty
Plenty be found within our borders
Let one and all arise
With hearts both strong and true
Service be our earnest endeavor
And our homeland of Kenya Heritage of splendor
Firm may we stand to defender.
Let all with one accord
In common bond united
Build this our nation together
And the glory of Kenya
The fruit of our labor
Fill every heart with thanksgiving.

From Egypt, originally in Arabic:

My homeland, my homeland, my homeland,
You have my love and my Heart.
My homeland, my homeland, my homeland,
You have my love and my Heart.

Egypt! O mother of all lands,
you are my hope and my ambition,
And above all people
Your Nile has countless graces

Egypt! Most precious gem,
A blaze on the brow of eternity!
O my homeland, be for ever free,
Safe from every enemy!

Egypt, land of bounties
You are filled with the ancient glory
My purpose is to repel the enemy
And on God I rely

Egypt, noble are thy children.
Loyal, and guardians of the reins.
Be we at war or peace
We will sacrifice ourselves for you, my country.

Dear Ayesha,

See how Africans cherish their God and their Land !

Until PANAFEST as an international festival became popular in Ghana, very few Ghanaians and Africans had visited the Slave forts and castles dotted across the central and west coasts of West Africa to educate themselves about the inhuman treatment meted out to fellow Africans by colonial rulers.

What happened at PANAFEST?

PANAFEST re-energized the African Unity dream. From all corners of the pan-African world came artistic performers, vendors, academics and intellectuals, traditional leaders, and enthusiastic youth joining together to celebrate African achievements as well as confront the pains and horrors of the slave trade.

Dear Ayesha,

At PANAFEST, there is an atonement ceremony led by the chiefs and people of Edina at the Elmina Castle. Apart from the Slave Route dotted around the country from North to South which is an option to track, intellectuals gather at a colloquium to discuss subject matters relating to the Rebirth of African Civilization; the Youth meet to discuss plans for 'Uniting the African Family''; women share experiences from across the continents, and there are exhibitions of arts and crafts open to merchandise.

Diaspora couples go through rituals for remarrying in the African tradition, or families are taken through re-naming ceremonies, as optional programmes. And the grand durbar of chiefs, performers, cultural manifestations crowns PANAFEST with statements from various delegations and the host country Ghana.

Dear Ayesha,

August 1st is marked as Emancipation Day with special activities, including a candle light vigil, in the Cape Coast Castle, and the celebration ends with a grand durbar of chiefs and people at Assin Manso Slave River site.

But that is not enough. What happens on the other side?

In 1994, I was invited by the publisher of the US edition of my book 'The Trial of JJ Rawlings', Halif Khalif Khalifah, on behalf of the Juneteenth Committee, to participate in activities marking the 375th anniversary of the Arrival of the First African in America, held in Jamestown and Hampton, in Virginia. Among other places of interest he took me to visit was the Nat Turner Library and Museum, which he managed.

Then in 2017, on a working vacation with my wife Nana in Virginia, USA, we toured the Jamestown Colony, parts of colonial Williamsburg, and listened to various versions of the history of the colony itself, as well as the story of the arrival of the first African in Fort Monroe, and settlement in Jamestown, near Hampton.

Old Fort in Jamestown, Virginia

My biggest treasure from the visit was a book I found : ***"The Birth of Black America: The First African Americans and the Pursuit of Freedom at Jamestown"***, written by Tim Hashaw.

Tim, a descendant of Jamestown's first Africans, did a great job as an outstanding investigative reporter and produced an excellent chronicle of what has been described by his publisher as 'the true tale of intrigue, piracy, slavery, and freedom surrounding the 1619 birth of black Africa'.

In the same year 2017, courtesy Dr Yvette Butler, my wife and I visited and toured the National Museum of African-American History and Culture, designed by a Ghanaian David Adjei, and established by the Smithsonian Institution in 2003 on the National Mall in Washington D.C. Yes, the diversity and richness of African culture, experiences and contributions to the building of the United States of America inspired me more to start writing.

Dear Ayesha,

The exact location for the first 20+ arrivals from Angola, Africa was Point Comfort, now Fortress Monroe, near Hampton, before they settled some 30miles away in Jamestown.

Over 10million Africans were taken away between the 16[th and] 19th century out of the continent by the Portuguese, the Dutch, the French, and the British from various ports such as Aneho, Ouidah, Lagos, Badagry, Porto-Novo, from Luanda in Angola, from Sene-Gambia, Guinea-Bissau, Guinea, Sierra Leone, Liberia, as well as from Elmina, Cape Coast, and **Jamestown** in the Gold Coast, now Ghana.

In this book, **Jamestown, Gold Coast** is used to represent the port of departure for all slaves of African descent, and as well represent the destination in **Jamestown**, Virginia in the United States of America, both locations named after King James 1 and King James 11 of England.

My dear Ayesha,

So, why **From Jamestown to Jamestown**?

In Ghana, I found Jamestown, a fishing port in Accra and a former trading outpost, to be ideal choice to represent the location from where to start the journey of African traded slaves to Jamestown in the Americas.

Of equal significance to me is the fact that Jamestown, Accra is where is found the **James Fort prison** where Dr Kwame Nkrumah was detained in 1951, in his struggle to lead Ghana to independence.

To understand the full essence of the search for the true identity of the African and the need for Africans to reunite with the rest of the Family, it is important to scan the elements which have lasted as African Civilization, take the infamous trip with slaves across the Atlantic, understand the sacrifices made by Africans toward the building of America, follow the Civil Rights Movement in the Americas and end with the Pan-Africanist ideas from which Kwame Nkrumah and other leaders emerged to light the torch for African liberation.

James Fort Prison, Jamestown, Accra

Dear Ayesha,

I have composed "**Letters to an African Child**", with reference to facts, books and documents that have been published over the years and which vividly describe the signposts and various episodes in the long journey we have taken to reunite with our kith and kin who were taken away from Africa more than 400 years ago.

"*From Jamestown to Jamestown - Letters to an African Child*" is education; it is history; it is life; it is African. It is Diaspora!

Dear Ayesha,

You are my African child. I chose you, **Ayesha**, because you symbolize **She who Lives**.

Dear Ayesha,

You are my pulse to the understanding of myself as African; you are my bridge between Africans on the continent and those in the diaspora, irrespective of their tribe, religion, faith or shade of colour.

As an instructive African proverb says:

"*Ignorance caused the chicken to go to sleep on an empty stomach, standing on a bag of corn!*"

Efo Kojo

Chapter 2

MUSINGS FROM JAMESTOWN CAFÉ, GHANA

"Despite the beauty of the moon, sun and stars, the sky also has threatening thunder and striking lightening" – African proverb

My dear Ayesha,

I am writing this letter from a unique hangout, called Jamestown café, overlooking the Atlantic Ocean, in Ghana, on the west coast of Africa. This haven is created by an African innovator-architect who is designing a new culture out of creative energies he intoxicates himself with from the everyday lives of fishermen and ordinary folk integrated with elites who patronize the joint. Joe Addo, an accomplished architect, has abandoned his original office in a plush area in the city of Accra and located his gallery and this pub among indigenous citizenry along the coast.

This is the corner which attracts creative actors – architects, journalists, educators, historians, musicians, designers, film makers, tourists – local and foreign, to share ideas, experiences, and stories about cultural development of Ghana and Africa, related to other experiences worldwide. Presentations are made on a wide variety of subjects and recorded weekly, and local food is served with relish.

Not far from the Café is situated the James Fort, which among other historical functions, was where Ghana's first president Osagyefo Kwame Nkrumah was kept in prison during the early fifties in the nationalist struggle for independence from British colonial rule. There is also the Ussher Fort which was named after a British governor Herbert Taylor Ussher when the British bought it from the Dutch in 1868.

At the Café, a historian and former mayor of Accra, Nat Nuno-Amarteifio, tells the history of Jamestown with the penchant of a griot:

'Fort James, as a fort, close to Jamestown Lighthouse, was built by the British as a trading post in Accra in 1673. Fort James gave its name to Jamestown, this neighborhood where is situated Jamestown Cafe.

It was named after King James of Great Britain who granted a royal charter to the Royal African company which later built the fort'.

Jamestown Café, Jamestown, Accra

Dear Ayesha,

I will later tell you more about this King James, after whom is named one version of the Christian Bible.

But, for now, historian Amarteifio narrates that Jamestown's cosmopolitan mix of peoples today started literally at its birth. Jamestown is a mixture of descendants of merchants, laborers, aristocrats, domestic slaves, fishermen, artisans and entrepreneurs from various parts of West Africa.

At the Jamestown Café, Kpakpo Bruce Allotey, a custodian of Jamestown folktale and epics, tells in one of his stories:

"There used to be Teiko, a replica of a modern heavyweight boxer who everybody feared in school. If you ever offended Teiko in school, he would ambush you after school behind the lighthouse and challenge you to a fight at the beach." And, by the way, the Jamestown neighborhood has produced some of the best boxers that ever came out of Africa.

"Teiko was not a terror at school", continues Allotey, *"but he hated lies and unjustified insults on his person"*.

Then there was Akwele, that 17year old quintessence of a beauty that all the aristocrats and merchants eyed. She walked gracefully on the streets of Jamestown after school knowing that there were all eyes on her; but she enjoyed having the likes of Teiko as friends to guard her. Daughter of King Okaikoi, she was conscious of her royal status, but she was scared that the king's wrath would descend on any man who dreamt or attempted to invade her virginity.

Occasionally, her friends who were children of merchants and who did not succeed in wooing her would tease her with "they say it was your father and his father King Manpong who sold our lands to the white man". To which she would respond angrily, "I will tell my father to excommunicate your family from here". And it was said the king exercised those powers in rare cases.

It was a taboo to say in public that the king was on the side of the Swedes, Dutch or British who fought over ownership of the castles and forts for slave and gold trading purposes. But it was also publicly known that some of the king's elders and the youth

45

openly protested against the actions of the king. Teiko, in spite of his occasional protection of Akwele was one such critic of the king.

Dear Ayesha,

Some 147 kilometers away on the coastline westwards, Elmina and Cape Coast portrayed the same features as Jamestown – cosmopolitan populations and bustling marketplaces for merchandise. Local agents for recruitment of human beings as domestic slaves and laborers were common. But more interestingly, the central coast of the then Gold Coast possessed the attractions that made many an explorer hungry to settle and trade.

The Elmina Castle was built in 1482 by the Portuguese who found a variety of kingdoms spread across the region. By the middle of the 17th century, the Danes and Dutch adventurers had taken over the trading activities and there was intense colonial rivalry among the invaders.

The Cape Coast Castle, few kilometres away from Elmina Castle, was a small trading lodge until 1637 when it was occupied by the Dutch. The Swedes captured it in 1652 and named it Fort Carlousburg, until after a series of wars the British took it over and renamed it Cape Coast Castle. It served as the seat of the British administration in the Gold Coast until 1877 when the capital of the Gold Coast was moved on 19th March, 1877 to the Christianborg Castle in Accra.

Until 1877, right under the Governor's Residence and a church, dungeons held over 1000 male captives and 500 female captives at any one time while waiting for between six and twelve weeks to be transported by one of the ships across the Atlantic Ocean. The treatment of the slaves in Cape Coast castle was the same as the fate suffered by all slaves from any part of Africa.

Dear Ayesha,

At Jamestown Café, the bar, local cuisine and African music, reggae and jazz have their own attractions and clientele; but vibrant formal and informal conversations on various topics and personalities on Africa constitute the essence of the spot. Africa's dying architectural monuments and relics are a concern for the patrons of the Café, and Joe Addo is always alive with his deep intellectual analysis of why Africa needs to be re-invigorated, beginning with the mindset. Did the white culture live too long on the coast of Africa to infest the population? And creativity died with the period of slavery and colonization?

Oh no, and what happened to all the original crafts and traditional games which portrayed the wisdom and strategic moves of the people.

Jamestown Café celebrates African genius and talent. The famous South African musician Hugh Masekela is a big favourite here. Before he died, he performed here a couple of times and his music is still played here. Musical performances by local community artistes are also common on most nights.

One evening, the discussions shifted to Angola, and Kwesi Welbeck, another historian, filled in the gaps, while Joe Addo served kelewele and fried yams with fish to match.

Dear Ayesha,

Greater Angola originally consisted of Bantu nations, like most of Africa in Central, Eastern and Southern regions. There were three nations – Bakongo, Mbundu and Ovimbundu. The Bantu Mbundu nations in Angola gave their kings the title of ngola (meaning iron blacksmith) to reflect their ability to manufacture iron several centuries before Europeans arrived on the coast of Africa.

Bantu culture introduced proverbs and Anansi folktales into Angola, and the people hunt with bows and arrows as in other parts of the continent. They rear cattle, goats, chickens and guinea-fowl, and are reputed to be hard working farmers. Long before European and Asian agriculture developed, the Bantu had produced carbonized steel.

It is customary in Angola for the bridegroom to give cattle as dowry for his bride, a common practice in other parts of Africa.

It was the Portuguese who gave trade names to most parts of Africa following the various expeditions their navigators undertook in the 14th and 15th centuries. So they named the Pepper Coast, the Ivory Coast, the Gold Coast, and the Slave Coast. They found, to their surprise, that unknown to their Mediterranean world, countries in the South Atlantic had an impressive advanced civilization – refining gold, silver, copper and iron.

There was the **Kongo Empire** – the size of Portugal, France and Germany combined.

Unlike other regions of Africa, Angola bore the brunt of mainly Portuguese and Spanish colonial expansionist ambitions.

Dear Ayesha,

So, why King James?

In 1603, an avid hunter and King of Scotland, was chosen to succeed Queen Elizabeth 1 of England. A young king of Scotland at the age of 13 months, he succeeded childless Queen Elizabeth 1 at the age of 36. Raised a Presbyterian, he changed course when he became King of England.

With his famous quote, 'No Bishop, No King', he responded to agitation from Reformists to order a new translation of the Bible , 'because those which were allowed in the reign of King Henry VVI and King Edward VI were corrupt and not answerable to the truth of the original''.

Earlier versions included the Tyndale, Matthew, the Bishops Bible, and the Geneva Bible (Presbyterian). It is said that the Geneva Bible had downplayed the divine right of Kings. Hence, the gathering of 50 language scholars and university professors to write the King James Version of the Bible.

It did not take long for King James to carry out a hidden plan – to unite England, Wales and Scotland as the United Kingdom. He is quoted to have told Parliament after his coronation: "What God hath conjoined then, let no man separate. I am the Husband, and all the whole Isle is my lawful Wife."

Dear Ayesha,

King James had another ambition: with the Church of England behind him, to limit the power of the Catholic Church and rule by absolutism – exercising the divine right to rule by decree. Known as the founder of the British Empire, King James had as pillars of his reign Absolutism, a United and centralized government, Colonization, and International peace and Trade.

Absolutism: all powerful, despot, dictator, one man rule, ruling by decrees.

United and Centralized government – against federalism, reign of terror.

Colonization – taking over and exercising absolute control over indigenous people of an area, including killing, driving away and exterminating indigenous people. It meant dominating their minds; destroying their culture.

International Peace and Trade – ensuring that an atmosphere was created for open exploitation with less opposition, particularly from Spain and Portugal, and from the colonized people.

Yes, that is King James, after whom is named a Version of the Bible.

That is King James, reported to have been a homosexual lover of the Earl of Buckingham, George Villiers, despite his known marriage to Anne of Denmark.

That is King James 1, who obsessed with witchcraft, wrote the book **"Daemonology"** – to convince doubters of the existence of witchcraft, and also to inspire those who persecuted witches to do so with vigor and determination.

Dear Ayesha,

There are records to show that the Royal African Company, chartered to supply slaves direct from Africa to the colonies, was deeply rooted in British society. The British royal family were among its principal shareholders, with King Charles's brother, the future James II of England and VII of Scotland, also taking a leading personal role in its management. William St. Clair, in his "Door of No Return" lists as other shareholders the Bishop of Oxford, the Earl of Lichfield, the Duke of Argyll, the Earl of Holderness, army and navy officers, gentlemen, churchmen, lawyers and many others.

My dear Ayesha,

Far away in Virginia, USA, three ships, Susan Constant, Godspeed and Discovery, owned by the Virginia Company of London had brought 104 Englishmen in 1606 to settle on a hunting land originally owned by the Powhatan Indian tribe, and called it Jamestown, after King James 1.

The settlers, afraid for their lives after driving the Indians away, and also to protect themselves from Spanish attacks, built a triangle-shaped fort surrounded on three sides by water. From then on, the Virginia Company shipped in more settlers, and appointed their government to consolidate their stay in the new colony.

History has it that strange diseases began attacking the settlers after only a few months after settling. Swellings, fevers, famine and fluxes took a toll on the settlers. When food was running low, it was the native Indians, led by their paramount chief, who came to the rescue of a dying colony. But then, relations got worse when the English settlers began demanding too much food from the Indians, which angered the locals.

The winter of 1609-10, known as the "Starving Time", saw a large number of settlers dying or living on any animal they could lay hands on, leather from their shoes and belts, and sometimes carcasses of their fellow men.

The settler numbers started growing when shipwrecked traders arrived from Bermuda and introduced **tobacco** as a cash crop. The Virginia Company of London saw the opportunity to make profit from their investments and therefore decided to concentrate on growing tobacco as a big business.

Dear Ayesha,

It is important to note that England was a relatively poor country in the 16th and 17th centuries. It was King James who gave Royal Charter to the Virginia Company of London in 1606 to pursue his colonization agenda. The company originally wanted gold and silver in Virginia – any raw materials they could lay hands on to pay the wealthy investors in London.

In July 1619, the Virginia Company's appointed Governor Yeardley established the first representative legislative assembly in Jamestown and recruited hundreds of women from England to marry the settlers.

It was around the same time that more ships were licensed by King James to bring in slaves from Africa to work on the tobacco plantations.

Of course, there are records of other Africans shipped by the Portuguese and Spanish traders to various parts of the world including the West Indies, Mexico, Bermuda, and even in South Carolina.

But, you know what, the slave trade had the same motive: to sell Africans to Europeans and other settlers to work on tobacco and cotton plantations to further economic interests.

Dear Ayesha,
Listen to Patrice Lumumba:
"We must sacrifice all that we have in order to teach and educate our children, for the future is in their hands'

I will get back to you soon.

Efo Kojo

Chapter 3

FROM PANAFEST TO JAMESTOWN, VA

'Return to old watering holes for more than water; friends and dreams are there to meet you' – African Proverb

My dear Ayesha,

You must find time to read more books about African heroes and heroines. Read about a famous author, playwright, child advocate, educator, dramatist and cultural activist who was born in Ghana in 1924 and died in 1996.

Efua Sutherland is her name. She was married to an African American, Bill Sutherland, who relocated to live in Ghana in the 1950s. She was a respected and highly recognized writer and Pan-Africanist in the circles of others you should read about - Ama Ata Aidoo, Maya Angelou, W. E. B. Du Bois and Shirley Graham du Bois, Margaret Busby, Langston Hughes, Martin Luther King and Coretta Scott King, Femi Osofisan, Felix Morisseau-Leroi, Es'kia Mphahlele, Wole Soyinka, Ngugi wa Thiong'o, and Chinua Achebe, among many others.

Dear Ayesha,

It was Efua Sutherland, who in a paper to the Government of Ghana in the late '80s proposed the establishment of the Pan-African Historical Theatre Festival of Arts and Culture (PANAFEST) to be the cultural vehicle for bringing Africans on the continent and those in the diaspora together to confront issues raised by slavery which had eroded the self-confidence of most black people. Originally started as a Drama Festival in the Cape Coast Castle in 1991, PANAFEST took a formal shape in 1992 and was launched by the Head of State at the time, Flight Lt Jerry John Rawlings. In his address, Flt-Lt Rawlings stated that the festival marked the beginning of a festival movement with its "great source of cultural enrichment for all Africans at home and abroad."

African chiefs pour libation for atonement

Dear Ayesha,

PANAFEST got bigger in 1994. As chairman of the Publicity Committee, I joined the then Executive Secretary, Akunu Dake to travel in the UK, USA and the Caribbean to drum up the need for all peoples of African descent to come to PANAFEST in July of that year.

With full support of the Government of Ghana, and the then Organization of African Unity (OAU) through Ghana's embassies abroad, we succeeded in inviting the world famous musician Stevie Wonder to launch the festival in Harlem, New York. The musical icon who flew to Ghana to chair the 1994 edition and perform said in his speech:

"We must take anything we have and everything we can offer, to make for a united Africa. Even though Africans are a diversified people with different languages and live in different places, Africans are originally one people and must not allow differences to affect their unification."

About 4,000 participants from 32 countries across the globe poured into Ghana and took part in the seven-day long activities. Early arrivals followed the slave route from cities and towns in the Northern Region of Ghana through Brong Ahafo and Ashanti Regions to Assin Manso where slaves were said to have had their last bath before they were transported to Elmina and Cape Coast Castles.

At Elmina, a big welcome ceremony was organized at which an atonement was pronounced by the chiefs of the area at the park in front of the Castle. After this ceremony, the gates of Elmina Castle were opened for a tour by participants.

The rest of the activities were held in the twin city, Cape Coast. An intellectual colloquium was held at the University of Cape Coast; the Youth had their own sessions; Women discussed their own issues at the University auditorium. At the PANAFEST 'village' itself, a trade bazaar with exhibits from various parts of the world was held.

Dear Ayesha,

Efua Sutherland saw only two editions of PANAFEST in 1992 and 1994 (she died in 1996 at the age of 71), and did not live long to see the festival flourish to be what it has grown to be today.

As part of activities for PANAFEST 1994, optional naming and traditional marriage ceremonies were organized in various locations around Elmina and Cape Coast.

Let me tell you, Ayesha, about the experience of Jerry and Brenda Smith and their daughter from California. Jerry, 52, was a university professor and Brenda, 40, was a social worker, both living in Compton City. They were married for 10 years, with one child, Louisa 10.

The Smiths registered to sign for the re-naming event. There were six such applicants registered by the PANAFEST Secretariat.

Dear Ayesha,

At this village gathering near Elmina, the Chief is seated with the Queenmother and Elders; he is resplendently clothed in Kente with the appropriate local royal sandals to match, and ready to perform the naming ceremony. Two of his Elders are in their late 70s and are sitting as advisors. In front of the Elders is a small table with one dessert plate on it.

On the opposite side of the Chief and Elders are gathered a crowd of spectators in the front row of which sat the 'new family members' to be traditionally named, including the Smiths. The Smiths in their new locally sewn fabrics sat close to their adopted 'parents', pre-arranged by PANAFEST Secretariat. They have been fully rehearsed by their new parents.

They had been asked questions like:
Who were your biological parents?
Where were you born?
On what day were you born?
After whom were you named?

Dear Ayesha,

With answers provided, they are now welcomed into their new African family and given a Clan (Ebusua) name; clan being the nucleus lineage grouping they belong to.

The stage is set. The spokesperson for the chief clears his throat, silence follows all around the assembly and he announces:

"Let us all pray for good wishes to come'. To which the crowd responds: "Let good wishes come".

Continues the spokesperson: "The Chief wishes me to announce that we are here today to welcome new arrivals into our community. They will come in groups. The first group of three will stand and they will come forward one at a time".

To which there is a loud acclamation of approval from the crowd. The Smiths stand and step forward with anxiety and dry smiles drawn over their faces

"We will now invite the Asona Ebusuapanyin Egya Antobam to present the parents of the new members", concluded Okyeame, beckoning Egya Antobam to take over.

Egya Antobam, accompanied by Nana Kofi and Obaapayin Ama Tawia hold the hands of Jerry Smith on each side and take one step forward near the Chief and Elders.

Okyeame opens a bottle of local gin, fills an empty glass, and recites as he pours the drink on bare ground:

"Earth God, come for a drink;

Ancestors, come for a drink;

All our Elders who have passed on, come for a drink.

Today is a great day; it is the day that you have brought into the family new arrivals that are joining our family. Give us wisdom, give us joy, give us love to enable us live peacefully with all those who are formally joining us today……. We pray for good health; we pray for long life; we pray for prosperity for them all."

Crowd responds in joyful unison: "Well said".

Parents of Professor Jerry Smith now present him officially:

"Our son from the Asona Ebusua, born on a Sunday is named after our late uncle who was a famous and rich salt merchant in Elmina. His name : Kwesi Baako. We chose Kwesi Baako because we see our son has the qualities that the rich merchant possessed; he is humble, he is affable, he has the royal features of Uncle Kwesi Baako, his forehead resembles that of Uncle Kwesi and we believe he is Uncle Kwesi's reincarnation. On top of it all, he was born on a Sunday."

Wild cheers greet this presentation, and Prof Jerry Smith is led to go down on his knees before the Chief and Elders for their blessing. The Chief lays his right hand on his head and prays for the blessing of all ancestors for him, asking that he tells the truth all his life to befit the status of Kwesi Baako after whom he is named.

He is reminded that the name given to him is a noble one, and that he has to live up to the expectation of his new family and the whole community.

"You are called Kwesi because you were born on a Sunday; the man you are named after was called Baako, which means the number 'one', because he was the only child of his parents. He worked so hard after school as an entrepreneur, that by the time he was 40 he ran a lucrative salt business and employed dozens of youth from this area. He left behind five children, some of who live outside Elmina. He is highly respected in this area".

Jerry was moved to hear all this coming from the chief and it sent tears down his cheeks. He felt humbled, and proud at the same time. His wife Brenda, and daughter Louisa followed suit and were also given local names. They left that PANAFEST activity with a unique feeling of joy mixed with emotion.

The PANAFEST evenings were reserved for theatre and concerts staged by performers from various parts of the world at various venues in Cape Coast and Elmina.

Dear Ayesha,

The climax of the usual PANAFEST event is the traditional gathering of all the chiefs and participants at the durbar grounds near the Cape Coast Castle.

This is where you saw the beauty and splendor of African traditional pomp and pageantry, the display of colorful rich woven kente, the symbolism in drum and dance language, the order and symmetry in regal procession, and the seamless blend of official and unofficial participation in a communal function. Speeches are programmed to match the rhythmic progression of a festival with character: Africans from all over the world celebrating their unity in warmth and happiness.

African Family united by common ancestry
Courtesy: Panafest Secretariat.

Diaspora Africans honored at PANAFEST:
Courtesy Panafest Secretariat

Next door is the Cape Coast Castle through which all the visiting diaspora Africans had done a tour to symbolize their Return to the homeland.

Cape Coast Castle.
Credit: Nii Ayikwei Hammond

My dear Ayesha,

That was the PANAFEST picture I carried with me to the 375th anniversary of the arrival of the first Africans in America, in Jamestown, Virginia, to which I had been invited.

There was an intellectual symposium at the University of Hampton on the first night where various historians narrated the circumstances and conditions of the Arrival in Fort Monroe and Jamestown.

The following day, on the beach of Jamestown, Virginia, were lined hundreds of canopies and chairs to accommodate about 5,000 participants who had travelled from all over the black world, mainly from the United States of America.

There was evident joy and a sense of respect for the occasion for which people came. There were book stands, vendors, eateries, bars and entertainment joints. There was music of all genres coming from mounted speakers.

When the moment came to turn attention to the ship that was sailing majestically on the sea toward the venue, anxiety and a sudden state of suspense gripped the entire audience. The re-enactment of the Arrival was simply stunning.

Ship Arriving

Dear Ayesha,

I was invited to join the officials on the podium to step out to meet the boat that ferried the '20+ Africans' from the ship to shore. It was an emotional moment. A group of performers from the Yoruba tradition stepped forward, with sweat on their bodies, drumming and singing to welcome the symbolic group of Africans landing on the soil of America.

It reminded me of the Cuban Santeria, the Haitian Vodun, the Brazilian Candomble, and the Shango of Trinidad and Tobago, or the Akom of Ghana. Libation was poured to the Oshun deity and all African ancestors, according to Yoruba religion and some incantation followed to signify welcome to the shores of America.

We followed the procession that paced gracefully to the park arranged for speeches and performances.

I was introduced as a Minister of State from Ghana and listed to speak, after the main welcome address by Governor Lawrence Douglas Wilder and other speeches by leaders of various delegations from the diaspora world. I learnt that Governor Wilder was the first elected African American to serve as governor of a US state since the Reconstruction of America.

Dear Ayesha,

I was learning very fast, sitting by the Governor and sharing information with him about Ghana, Nkrumah and African liberation. When it was my turn to take the microphone I sent fraternal greetings from the continent of Africa, and specifically from Ghana where we had celebrated the second edition of the Pan-African Historical Theatre Festival; I expressed joy to be continuing the search for commonality in the international movement for uniting the African family.

I spoke about Kwame Nkrumah's vision, along with other pan-Africanists' determination, to see a United States of Africa.

I attracted attention for the simple reason that I came all the way from Ghana to attend the ceremony, and I mentioned Kwame Nkrumah whose name resonated among all the participants; and I shook as many hands as they were stretched to me.

There were other delegates from Embassies of some African and Caribbean countries and others from different cultural groups based in the United States of America.

Various musical performances, poetry recitals, dances and merry-making continued far into the night. My thoughts ran back towards the main theme of **PANAFEST: The Rebirth of African Civilization.**

Dear Ayesha,

Have you heard of **Emancipation Day** in Africa?

On August 1st, 1834, the British Governor in the Gold Coast, now Ghana, read a proclamation that announced the official abolition of chattel slavery in the British colonies. This proclamation was read in the precincts of Cape Coast Castle.

It was the Caribbean Historical Society of Trinidad & Tobago under Makandal Daaga, in 1969, that determined that the day should be commemorated throughout the world, particularly in the Caribbean and on the continent of Africa and in the black world, as a spiritual reawakening to say 'Never Again".

The Society raised awareness among the Caribbean people during the 1980s and lobbied the Government of Trinidad and Tobago to declare the day as a national holiday to replace the hitherto Columbus Discovery Day. I was to be a guest speaker much later in 2012.

The commemoration combined a night of vigil where prayers were said to the ancestors, and religious songs sang, with street processions and cultural activities, climaxed by inspiring speeches by the President and other invited dignitaries at the national stadium.

Dear Ayesha,

From 1985, after the successful first celebration of Emancipation Day in Port of Spain, Emancipation Day spread to Barbados, Guyana, Dominica and Jamaica, all under the active influence of the National Joint Action Committee of the Caribbean Historical Society in Trinidad and Tobago.

In 1997, the Prime Minister of Jamaica, Hon. P.J. Patterson, invited the then President of the Republic of Ghana, Flight Lieutenant Jerry John Rawlings to be the special guest of the Government and People of Jamaica on the commemoration of August 1st as Emancipation Day in Jamaica.

Before his return to Ghana, President Jerry John Rawlings accepted an invitation to visit Trinidad and Tobago. While in Trinidad, a delegation led by Brother Ome, then chairman of the National Joint Action Committee presented the Ghanaian President with a letter calling on the Government of Ghana to follow the lead of the Caribbean countries and declare 1st August as Emancipation Day in Ghana.

Dear Ayesha,

On his return to Ghana, President Jerry John Rawlings instructed the then Deputy Minister of Tourism, Honorable Owuraku Amofah, who accompanied him to the Caribbean, to team up with me as Minister of the Central Region and Chairman of PANAFEST to chair a National Preparatory Committee for the organization of Emancipation Day in Ghana.

Supported by Brother Obika of the National Action Committee of Trinidad and Tobago who had arrived in Ghana, the PANAFEST Secretariat, based in Cape Coast, organized for the first time in West Africa Emancipation Day 1998.

Dear Ayesha,

This was a unique moving experience.

On July 31st, 1998, Ghanaian officials welcomed the arrival by air of the remains of two relatives of slave ancestors from the

United States and Jamaica. Accompanied by a large delegation of Government and PANAFEST officials and the diaspora community, the caskets, carrying Samuel Carson and Crystal from the United States and Jamaica respectively, were received and driven by road to Kormantse, on the Accra-Cape Coast road.

The stopover at Kormantse was significant for two reasons: one, to enable the chiefs and people of the area to pour libation to receive Crystal from the 'Cormantins' of Jamaica, and second, to travel the rest of the journey to Cape Coast by fishing canoes.

The spirits of ancestors known for militarism, bravery, spirituality and power were invoked at the short ceremony, after which hundreds of people joined the 50 or more canoes flying African and Caribbean flags paddled in military formation on the sea to the edge of Cape Coast Castle, some 50 kilometers away.

My dear Ayesha,

Tears rolled down cheeks as thousands of participants and spectators poured onto the precincts of the Castle to watch the caskets of the two ancestors lowered down canoes and carried shoulder high through the now re-designated **Door of Return** into the courtyard.

After the necessary welcome libations, speeches and tributes, arrangements were made to convey the remains to Assin Manso, a town about 55 kilometers away on the Cape Coast-Kumasi road for reburial. Assin Manso had been earmarked as the last transit point where slaves were said to have had their last bath before their final condemnation to the Cape Coast or Elmina Castles.

As a final event to mark the first Emancipation Day commemoration in Ghana on 1st August 1998, a huge assembly of celebrants was organized at Assin Manso.

Hundreds of mourners made up of African Americans, other Africans from the diaspora and Ghanaians flocked the burial grounds at the site of the former slave river to pay their respects to the two ancestors.

The remains of the two ancestors, Carson and Crystal, were formally handed over to Obarima Nana Kwame Nkyi, Omanhene (paramount chief) of Assin Apimanim traditional area and were laid in state amidst loud drumming and the singing of funeral dirges.

Dear Ayesha,

Read a news agency report:

"Speaking at the durbar, Nana Akuoko Sarpong, Presidential Staffer on Chieftaincy Affairs, said the re-burial of the two signified a new chapter in the **atonement** process. Nana Akuoko Sarpong further said the event also served as a symbol of honour to all who struggled for the emancipation of all people of African descent, adding:'we are combining mourning with appreciation of the gallantry of the sufferers and fighters'.

"Nana Akuoko Sarpong pointed out that the history of Africans 'will not be complete without a coherent record of past events' and that it is the responsibility of this generation to record such events from which many lessons can be drawn. He said there is also the need to give "a revolutionary push" to the next stage of the struggle towards socio economic and industrial reconstruction of Africa.

" In his short remarks, Central Regional Minister and Chairman of PANAFEST Mr Kojo Yankah stressed the need for Africans on the continent and those in the Diaspora to cement their ties and together build a strong African family.

"Mr Minion Phillips and Mr Sonny Carson, relatives of the two ancestors, described the event as **''a home coming for all peoples of African descent".**

Candlelight procession at the Cape Coast Castle to mark Emancipation Day. Credit: Panafest Secretariat

Dear Ayesha,

It was the founder of the Caribbean Historical Society, Makandal Daaga of Trinidad & Tobago who said:

'History has taught us that Emancipation is not distinctly National or Racial, but it is a continuing process that involves all men and women of conscience'.

Emancipation, as you probably are realizing, is not limited to only one corner of the world. Just as blacks continue to pursue all means to emancipate and free themselves, it will be instructive for people of other colors, particularly whites, to free themselves of prejudices drummed in their minds by their teachers, books, ancestors and parents.

With Love
Efo Kojo

Cowries from Africa found at Jamestown, VA
Courtesy: Diallo Sumbry

Chapter 4

WHEN THE LIGHTS SHONE

'If we stand tall it is because we stand on the shoulders of many ancestors' – **African Proverb**

My dear Ayesha,

African history was not important to Europeans who invaded the continent and divided the continent among themselves for economic reasons. They knew that Egypt was the origin of all civilizations. They were aware that Egypt civilization lasted thousands of years and gave the world the science of medicine, mathematics, technology and the arts. Europeans knew that by the time the city of Rome was built, Egyptian civilization was in existence.

The Empire of Ghana, covering most of present French West Africa, was about the size of Europe, and this was known to the adventurers who called themselves discoverers. Europeans knew that Africa had very organized empires trading in gold, salt and copper. Rulers controlled well organized armies, and the ruler of the Ghana empire had an army of more than 200,000 men.

Dear Ayesha,

It was known to the Europeans that as far back as 500BC (before Christ), the Ife civilization was alive and trading in bronze, copper, wood and ivory. The Kingdoms of Benin and Ife were powerful in the 11th and 12th centuries, and the people were skilled in ivory carving, pottery, rope and gum production.

Yes, the Europeans were aware that the Kingdom of Mali spread 2000 kilometer wide across much of West and North East Africa, and that the people traded in gold dust and exported agricultural produce up north.

Oh yes, Europeans certainly knew that between 1450-1550, the Songhai Empire was a very powerful and prosperous kingdom, boasting of Timbuktu as a world center for trade and scholarship.

Dear Ayesha,

Yes, there was African civilization. Yes, we have every right to be proud of our African ancestors.

A rather notorious lie has been peddled that Africans were not used to writing, that every piece of communication was oral, and that is why you hear the uninformed insulting remark that 'if you want to hide anything from the African put it in a book".

I have read the book entitled **"When We Ruled"** by Robin Walker, a well-researched masterpiece; I have read well-documented published books by Senegalese Cheikh Anta Diop, especially the two entitled **"Civilization or Barbarism"** and **"The African Origin of Civilization"**.

I have delved into publications by Molefi Kete Asante, particularly **"The History of Africa"** and **"The Egyptian Philosophers"**, and I have enjoyed reading **"The Stolen Legacy"** by George James; and there are dozens of researched materials of black scholars.

Dear Ayesha,

I am convinced beyond doubt that our educational system since the colonial days has totally imprisoned us and made us enemies of ourselves.

Our education has taught us to despise who we are, what we have, and everything we can refer to as African. We hate our culture; we do not want to know our true identity, and we enjoy going about as caricatures in borrowed robes.

There is an African proverb which clearly states:

"You cannot smile with somebody else's teeth".

How true !

Or again:

"You cannot fly with someone else's wings".

How can we Africans think, develop our God-given talents, and create a better future for ourselves if we continue to believe and see ourselves as inferior to some other race and behave as if we believe we have no history.

Dear Ayesha,

The good news is that you and your generation have the unique opportunity to liberate your minds. And I believe you will certainly be different!

Records are available to show that our ancestors wrote a lot of books and that there were deliberate efforts by invaders to **destroy** or **hide** them. Even then, more than 3,000 hand-written medieval books have been found to have been written in two Mauritanian cities of Chinguetti and Oudane, and that the city of Walata had twice the number of books, dating back to the 8th century AD.

And then there are over 700,000 books in private libraries in Mali and Niger surviving since the 8th century. Architectural edifices in the city of Benin in West Africa and in Mogadishu in East Africa have been confirmed by 15th century Chinese records as having existed to show the scientific skills Africans possessed.

Dear Ayesha,

The Ancient Kongo Empire I mentioned earlier covered Angola, Gabon and the two Congos before the invasion of Portuguese and Spanish colonialists, long before King Leopold of Belgium claimed it as his property, and the people still exhibit their manufacturing skills and cultural prowess. And of course, it is because of the rich minerals in that area that wars have existed for centuries, even after the so-called independence from Europeans.

In Nigeria, the ancient sculptures of the civilization of Ile-Ife still exist, just as the Kingdom of Ashanti in Ghana, despite all the stolen crats and jewelry kept in European museums. The Shona civilization of the people of Zimbabwe and parts of Southern Africa has contributed to the resilience of the people despite onslaughts by modern day apostles of democracy.

The royal architecture of Dahome (now Benin) is still alive and there is much to learn about the great Empires of Ghana, Songhai and Mali.

Dear Ayesha,

Africa had the first university in the whole world. The University of Timbuktu (in Mali) in the 15th century produced hundreds of scholars, as has been confirmed by British historian and Oxford scholar Thomas Hodgkin in an article he published in The Highway as recently as 1952.

By the way, Ayesha, the University of Timbuktu was located in three mosques (campuses) – in Sankore, Djinguereber, and Sidi Yahya, in the city of Timbuktu in what is now Mali. At one time, student enrolment was 25,000 in a city whose population was 100,000.

Subjects taught included Law, Literature, Science, Mathematics, and Medicine, but it was most popular for its curriculum termed Circle of Knowledge which was taught across all the stages of schooling.

It is known that scholars and historians of the 17th century have recorded a high number of doctors, judges, clerics and philosophers coming out of this university.

Dear Ayesha,

Timbuktu was not only the center of the academic world, it was also described as the epicenter of global trade routes following the Niger River. Gold was in abundance here and it was traded between Europe and what is now known as Mali.

Yes, that is where Arabs, the Tuaregs, the Fulani, and the Wangara met to trade. It is on record that several centuries before Columbus ever set sail, a well known Malian, named Abubakar II, had travelled from Timbuktu to the Americas trading.

During the 11th century, Timbuktu was referred to as the cross-roads where 'the camel met the canoe'.

Timbuktu University

My dear Ayesha,

There is a reason why the United Nations Educational, Scientific and Cultural Organization (UNESCO) in 1988 granted Timbuktu the world heritage site status.

Timbuktu's importance as a world centre of learning is a fact. UNESCO has found over 700,000 manuscripts from the medieval era which are being digitized so that the world can continue to learn that Africa was the center of world scholarship.

There are available in the UNESCO monument, which includes the University of Timbuktu, manuscripts and books on law, literature, religion, science, commerce, chemistry, physics, geography, astronomy, Islamic sciences and traditions, jurisprudence and mathematics. Added to the world heritage lists are 16 cemeteries and mausoleums.

Dear Ayesha,

I will recommend to you and all African youth to visit the world heritage site in present day city of Timbuktu.

You will be welcomed by staff of the Timbuktu Educational Foundation who will show you how black Africa has been robbed of its pride and honor through slavery and colonialism. They will tell you why the continent was labelled the Dark Continent after the pillage of its heritage.

You will learn about the thousands of African and European scholars and political leaders who received their education from the University of Timbuktu, once the world's center of learning and a symbol of African civilization.

The British scholar Hodgkin has admitted that, "The thesis that Africa is what Western European missionaries, traders, technicians and administrators have made it is comforting to Western Europeans, but **invalid**." (Quoted in JC De Graft Johnson, **African Glory**, UK Watts & Co. 1954)

As a matter of fact, when the Europeans arrived on the continent of Africa at the turn of the 15th Century, they destroyed all the rich kingdoms they met, some of which were the Mwene Mutapa Empire and the kingdoms of the African East Coast.

It is also true that Arab invaders and their allies ransacked parts of the East Coast and along the Sahara and imposed their religion on parts of the North and East Africa.

Dear Ayesha,

What has been missing from the African story is that the viewpoints have always come from Europeans who wrote about our continent. They were assisted by some of our African historians who had to pass their examinations at the hands of these same Western scholars of old. But gradually, the truth is coming out.

In a book authored by Yosef A.A. Ben-Jochannan, entitled Africa, Mother of Western Civilization, and published in 1971 by US Black Classis Press, Dr Victor Robinson confesses quite clearly:

"It is one of the paradoxes of history that Africa, the Mother of Civilization, remained for over two thousand years the Dark

Continent…..In the time of Jonathan Swift (1667-1745), as the satirist informs us, geographers in drawing maps fill in the gaps with savage pictures. Where towns should have been, they placed elephants".

My dear Ayesha,

I hope you understand clearly that the term 'The Dark continent" was deliberately coined to cover the technology, science and intellectual pride of Africa which they were bent on either destroying or appropriating.

They drew the maps and portrayed our continent as savage. It was as if the continent was populated by only wild animals. That is how they wanted the rest of the world to view us: and to a large extent they succeeded, because when we were 'Christianized' we believed everything we were told through the education we received.

Pyramid of Giza, a World wonder in Egypt

75

Dear Ayesha,

You certainly have heard of the Pharaohs in the Bible.

Yes, the **Pharaoh** was the supreme ruler of the people of Egypt. He was considered the intermediary between the gods and the people. To the Egyptians, he was a god on earth, associated with Horus, the god who had defeated the forces of chaos and restored order. When a Pharaoh died, he was associated with Osiris, the god of the dead.

Certainly, you have heard or read about the Great Pyramids of Egypt. When I was in school, I was taught that they were designed and built by the Greeks and

Romans when they conquered Egypt. Nothing could be farther from the truth. They were built by Africans.

In Ethiopia and Egypt are found some of the oldest excavations of the origin of man, and there is abundant evidence that blacks populated all those areas in Ethiopia and Egypt where world civilization began.

Famous Senegalese historian and scholar Cheikh Anta Diop, in **Great African Thinkers**, Vol 1, 1986, confirms the typically **negroid** features of the Pharaoh dynasties, including that of Cheops (Khufu), the builder of the Great Pyramid. From the source of the Nile River came our ancestors who are described as the original human beings as we know today.

Dear Ayesha,

If you did not know, I want to let you understand that Christianity did not come from the Jews or Judaism who have a claim to the Old Testament. (Sometimes I wonder why our people go on Christian pilgrimages to Israel).

Christianity came from the Nile region, the original home of spirituality, from where we will learn Islam also came from.

You know St Paul? He wrote the Gospels to the Romans, Galatians, the Thessalonians, and the Ephesians to convert them.

There certainly was a reason for the Romans and English, after invading Egypt, to link the Old Testament to the New Testament.

Reading the very well written published work of Cheick Anta Diop, entitled 'Civilization or Barbarism' and others, I learn that the word **Christ** does not come from the Greek Language 'christos' as was taught in our high school days; it is rooted in the pharaonic tradition, and that is why no one in the Hebrew tradition has called himself Christ.

Dear Ayesha,

Let me tell you an interesting story. There was the god of Osiris (sometimes called Isis) in ancient Egypt. He was described as someone 'who did good, who suffered, who died and rose again and ascended into heaven and his blood had to be drunk'.

So in the Pyramid of Unas, you read this: "Drink, this is the blood of Osiris, this is his flesh". Is it just a coincidence?

And again, you read in the worship of Osiris (Isis) about baptism, public confession, incarnation of God made man, who died for the redemption of human kind, and his resurrection from the dead. Could this also be coincidental?

So did Christ come from Egypt? If not, did his stay in Egypt give him the opportunity to acquire his spirituality?

Whatever, it is, I believe we blacks have a reason to claim Jesus Christ as an African.

My dear Ayesha,

It is not a secret that the first inhabitants of Palestine, then called Canaan, were blacks. Issa and Meri are pharaonic names.

History tells us again that Emperor Constantine, after the invasion of Egypt in the 4th century, ordered the destruction of temples and replaced them with churches. That was when it is recorded that he imposed the white figure of Jesus Christ as the one created by St Paul of Tarsus.

Education continues, Ayesha.

Dear Ayesha,

Africa really had kingdoms and empires. Nubia, Axum, Ghana, Mali, Songhay. Read more about the Kemet and Kush Kingdoms.

Read about Carthage, which Molefi Kete Asante calls "Africa's Mediterranean powerhouse". There is so much written by Arab historians such as Ibn Battuta, Ibn Khaldun, Leo Africanus, that was hidden from us.

Oh yes, there were the golden eras of the Empires of Ghana, Mali, Kanem-Borno in the region of Lake Chad. There have been the booming economies of the Hausa, and the religion and art of Yoruba states and Akan kingdoms.

There are interesting similarities about the religions of Yoruba and Akan in their concept of God and various attributes: There is one Supreme Being; Ancestors must be honored, respected and consulted; Your spirit lives after death and can reincarnate through blood relatives; Character is the greatest trait of the human being.

Dear Ayesha,

I find the logic in the words of Catholic Archbishop Dr Akwasi Sarpong who writes in his book "**Libation**":

'Prayer is a kind of instinctive cry from the human soul to a power the person believes is higher and implies that the power can be of help in time of need and on other occasions'.

The venerable archbishop is emphatic that Christianity has come to fulfil African traditions: 'Therefore Christianity cannot abolish a cultural institution...To abolish an innocuous age old practice like libation is to destroy the philosophy of the life of the people and their very ethos'.

Dear Ayesha,

There lived a Ghanaian journalist and writer, J.E. Casely-Hayford, who wrote in the 1950s : 'I would lay stress upon the fact that while Ramses II was dedicating temples to the God of gods...the God of the Hebrews had not yet appeared to Moses in the burning bush; and that Africa was the cradle of the world's systems and philosophies and the nursing mother of its religions. Africa has nothing to be ashamed of in its place among the nations of the earth.'

Dear Ayesha,

South American historian and author, George G.M. James, is categorical in his famous book, **"Stolen Legacy",** that there is no philosophy as Greek Philosophy, from which the world has been fed for so long. It is a misnomer, he emphasizes.

The Greeks, when they invaded Egypt after five thousand years, stole the very complex Egyptian religious system called the **Mysteries**, known to be the first system of salvation, and the basis of all ethical concepts. Through the Persian invasion, and that of Alexander the Great, from the sixth century to the death of Aristotle, the Greeks were permitted to learn about the Mysteries and Egyptian culture from Egyptian priests.

Dear Ayesha,

According to George James, Aristotle learnt from the Greeks after the invasion of Alexander the Great, when the school of Aristotle converted the royal temples and libraries into a research center.

The Greeks borrowed their study of Ethics from the Egyptian 'Summum Bonum', or the greatest good. And the command, **Know Thyself,** attributed to Socrates and Plato, by western intellectuals, were inscriptions copied from Egyptian temples for neophytes.

The four cardinal virtues taught for centuries in the western world and carried to schools and universities, Justice, Wisdom, Temperance and Courage, were all copied by Plato from Egyptians in North Africa.

My dear Ayesha,

Since the Egyptian Mystery System was the first secret Order of History, and its publication prohibited, initiates like Socrates could not commit to writing.

It is affirmed by George James that it was the Egyptians who taught Pythagoras and the Greeks what has become known as the Pythagoras Theory. James makes it clear that his aim for the extensive research and publication of his book, **Stolen Legacy** is to show that 'this theft of the African legacy by the Greeks led to the erroneous world opinion that the African continent has made no contribution to civilization, and that its people are naturally backward.'

Dear Ayesha,

This has become the basis upon which whites have built their race superiority and supported slavery, colonization, apartheid and all forms of indignities and disrespect against blacks in the name of God.

Dear Ayesha,

Note this Ethiopian proverb:

"The kingdom of heaven is within you; and whomsoever shall know shall find it".

The Akan in Ghana say in a proverb:

"Knowledge of God is innate".

Wiping out ignorance takes time, but we will get there.

In November, 2016, Ghanaian philosopher Anthony Kwame Appiah shook the airwaves and the academic world by stating in the BBC Reith Lecture series: **"There is no such thing as western civilization".**

I could feel the number of academics and intellectuals, not least from Africa, trembling and wondering; but, that is a truth we have to live with.

As John Henrik Clarke writes,

"Egypt gave birth to what later would become known as 'Western Civilization' long before the greatness of Greece and Rome".

There is more to follow, Ayesha.
Efo Kojo

Chapter 5

INSIDE THE DUNGEONS

"Any time I hear anyone arguing for slavery, I feel a strong impulse to see it tried on him personally' – Abraham Lincoln, March 17, 1865

'Any time anyone is enslaved, or in any way deprived of his liberty, if that person is a human being, as far as I am concerned he is justified to resort to whatever methods necessary to bring about his liberty again' – Malcolm X, Oxford Union debate, December 13, 1964.

My dear Ayesha,

Very few Africans have really toured the forts and castles dotted across the coasts of Africa. Even if they did, it is in recent times that well trained tour guides interpret more appropriately the story of the African.

Some stories told in the past were not different from the ones read in history books that made it seem as if Europeans were doing a lot of good to Africans who were so poor and uneducated that they needed to be Christianized.

In Ghana, interest in the castles arose after independence when a number of diaspora blacks were invited to Ghana to support the newly won independence. Even then, the civil rights movement in

America was still busy. In recent times, a lot of interest has been shown in castles and forts since activities

Cape Coast Castle overlooking the Atlantic Ocean

like PANAFEST brought peoples of African descent to the Elmina and Cape Coast castles.

Opportunity has been given to hear the horrid stories about how chained human beings were treated in dungeons unfit for the worst crimes in human history.

Occasionally one has come across the argument that slavery was not 'new' and that Africans were already doing it 'and so what'? Of course, people were, and are still, confusing the English word 'slave' with what in local language means 'servant' (*osomfo* in Akan). Otherwise a male slave was *akoa in Akan;* and female slave *afenaa.* Probably the closest English terminology is 'indentured servant'. He had rights, he could get married, and could even inherit property. He was NOT chained.

Of course, there were prisoners of war in Africa, due to inter-tribal wars. Yes, people were used as pawns for debts owed until debts were paid. Yes, people paid a price for crimes committed.

Dear Ayesha,

When Europeans arrived, they were looking for strong African men and women who would be transported across the seas to various parts of the world to fight their wars or to labor in their new plantations and economic ventures they had created for profit. Yes, they used African merchants and chiefs and paid them to find appropriate candidates.

The method of chaining human beings, making it impossible for them to escape or run away from their original abodes to the 'slave' markets and eventually to the forts and castles, was dictated by the European masters. This was what was called 'chattel slavery' – the state of being condemned, non-human, without any rights, and branded as such. This captive could be sold as property, traded, and passed on as inheritance.

This is where the horror began – they were bought, chained and dragged to the castles and forts and prepared for transportation on the Atlantic Ocean to the Americas and the Caribbean.

Dear Ayesha,

What exactly happened in the castle?

In most cases, the castle was the residence of the Governor. He lived in an airy and spacious suite on the top floor, with his top officials in the next rooms, overlooking the courtyard where the dungeons were located.

On the same top floor was a church where the governor and officials worshipped. On one of the church doors is an inscription from Psalm 132:

The Eternal Dwelling of God in Zion

'Lord, remember David, and all his afflictions" (King James Version)

'For the Lord has chosen Zion; he has desired it for his habitation;

This is my rest forever; here will I dwell; for I have desired it;

I will abundantly bless her provision; I will satisfy her poor with bread. His enemies will I cloth with shame; but upon himself shall his crown flourish".

Governor's Room overlooking the courtyard

Dear Ayesha,

Below the church and the governor's suite is the female dungeon. It is well known that the Governor usually looked down the courtyard from his balcony and selected African women he considered very beautiful, pointed at them, and invited them to have sex with him.

His officers copied the practice and raped most of the women. Some women who got pregnant were declared freed to go home, wherever they came from.

In a book, quoted by William St. Clair in his "The Door of No Return", the Castle chaplain Rev. Thomas Thompson writes in 1772 in dedication to the Company of Merchants, that "The African Trade for Negro Slaves is shown to be consistent with the Principles of Humanity and the Laws of Revealed Religion".

Reverend Thompson assures his readers that 'the slave trade had full biblical, Christian, and ecclesiastical endorsement – and that it was also part of the famed English national Liberty".

Dear Ayesha,

That is the interpretation of 'slavery' from the Governor and his Chaplains who supervised the Africans in slavery.

That explains why there were the dark 14x16 ft dungeons in which over 200 captives were kept at a time for between eight and twelve weeks before embarking upon that ignominious journey to the Americas or the Caribbean.

The Tunnel for all slaves to the waiting canoe.
Credit: Nii Ayikwei Hammond

Without water or lights, these poorly ventilated and dank spaces, littered with human excreta, were the only choice for human beings who were recruited to serve an economic purpose for their masters. In the male dungeons, the numbers were higher, more than 500 in one room. Food was handed through iron gates on a long paddle.

Call it Indignity! Humiliation! Torture! These words are not adequate to describe the treatment given to Africans who otherwise were leading their own peaceful lives in various parts of the continent.

Then there is the **Door of No Return**, behind which slaves were told that they would no longer come back to their native land. And the Europeans indeed wrote those words! Door of No

Return! Yes, the arched gateway with a pair of thick doors that said goodbye to the captured men, women and children of Africa.

So, where was the Christianity the Europeans announced they were bringing to the people?

And what if a captive rebelled? And a number of them certainly rebelled against these conditions. The response was immediate: transfer to the condemned cell – a smaller room with one hole in the wall for ventilation. As punishment, those who caused unrest could also be brought out and chained to one of the many canon balls in the courtyard.

Dear Ayesha,

Listen to a few lines from a story by a Ghanaian woman, Erica Ayisi, who lived in America and visited one of the castles:

"I entered the castle a bit numb. I knew what to expect – dark dungeons amidst a vast ocean. However, on first sight of the sign 'Female Slave Dungeon', my numbness quickly waned. Walking toward the scantily lit room, the smell of menstruation and human defecation grew paramount".

After 400 years, the stench still meets you even now. And Erica is right: *"As a woman I cannot be numb to such an inhumane aspect of history. The smell won't let me."*

Shout Terrible! Scream Horrible! That is the reality about the conditions under which Africans were made to feel **inferior**. It was part of the deliberately planned process of letting Africans feel they had no value.

Dear Ayesha,

The **New York Times** article of November 25, 1990 by Judith Graham puts it candidly: *"The history of these bastions ....is one of exploration, exploitation, greed and freedom lost. In their damp dungeons, the unimaginable becomes real"*.

Claudia Schank from Germany comments in the Visitor's Book at the Elmina Castle: *"How can people treat each other like that?"*

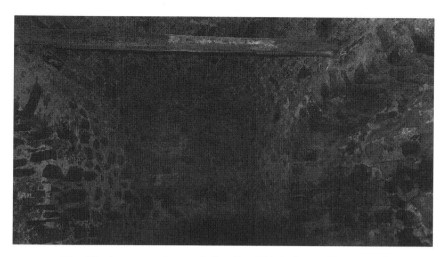

The Underground tunnel Credit: Nii Ayikwei Hammond

Yes, it happened. Judith Graham writes further about the underground tunnels: "An underground tunnel, through which slaves passed when they left the castle to waiting canoes, sweats with dampness. The peeling walls are covered with a green mold... Turning back along the tunnel to visit the male dungeons...I felt a swelling sense of oppression".

My dear Ayesha,

Do find time to visit one of the castles and forts on the west coast of Africa.

Invite your friends and go together. Your sentiments will not be different from what everybody expresses:

In the **Los Angeles Sentinel** of August 27, 2009, Assistant Managing Editor Yusuf Simmons, who visited one of the slave castles, had this to publish:

"It is virtually impossible to write about the Slave Castles without describing the brutality of the African slave trade, the most evil and insidious holocaust of Black human beings in history which was perpetrated primarily by white Europeans on Black African men, women and children. It was not only the physical being that was captured and destroyed, it was the mind, soul and spirit of millions of Black people who were uprooted and transplanted".

Dear Ayesha,

The sentiments are the same everywhere.

When Jacques Wallace toured the Dungeons in 2014, she could only tell CNN:

"I am slightly numb actually; I wasn't actually ready for the stories about this place as far as the way people were treated, and the thing about the tunnel and everyone bound and being led down the tunnel is a little bit tragic, a little bit too much to take in all at once

Exit to waiting boats.
Credit: Paa Kwesi Inkumsah

And her traveling companion Monique Ross wrote:

"It's devastating…It's good to know the history of what has happened and how to connect your historical past with things that have happened."

Dear Ayesha,

Search for and read the works of Maya Angelou. She was one of the most celebrated American writers. An African American, she was a poet, singer, actress, and civil rights activist. She died in 2014 at the age of 86.

She lived and worked in Ghana for about four years in the early '60s when Dr Kwame Nkrumah opened up Ghana to all peoples of African descent.

Once when she visited the 'slave' dungeons, Maya wrote:
"Africa is a historical truth...no man can know where he's going unless he knows exactly where he's been and exactly how he arrived at his present place."

Visitors coming out of dungeon.
Credit: Nii Ayikwei Hammond

Dear Ayesha,

Before her death in 2014, Maya, after another visit to Ghana, had composed this poem entitled **"All God's Children Need Traveling Shoes"**:

Maya Angelou

'I stopped at Cape Coast only for gas
Although many black Americans had headed for the town as soon
as they touched the ground in Ghana.
I successfully avoided it for a year.
Cape Coast Castle and the nearby Elmina Castle had been holding
forts for captured slaves.
The captives had been imprisoned in dungeons beneath the
massive buildings,
And friends of mine who had felt called upon to make the trek
reported that they felt the thick stone walls still echoed with old
cries.
I allowed the shapes to come to my imagination:
Children passed tied together by ropes and chains,
Tears abashed, stumbling in dull exhaustion;
Then women, hair uncombed, bodies gritted with sand, and
sagging in defeat.
Men, muscles without memory, minds dimmed, plodding, leaving
bloodied footprints in the dirt.
The quiet was awful.
None of them cried, or yelled, or bellowed.

No moans came from them.
They lived in a mute territory, dead to feeling and protest.
These were the legions, sold by sisters, stolen by brothers, bought
by strangers;
Enslaved by the greedy and betrayed by history. "

Visitors inside Cape Coast Castle
Credit: Nii Ayikwei Hammond

Dear Ayesha,

I have visited the Castles more than 20 times. I have toured with friends, Ghanaian and non-Ghanaian, tour groups, university teachers and students.

I have seen the 'slave' dungeons, on some occasions using torchlights to provide light; I have been in the governor's suite and looked down the courtyard; I have walked the extension overlooking the Atlantic Ocean displaying the armory that defended the occupants of the castle.

I have walked down the chapel. Down in the basement, I have watched closely the tunnel through which human beings were pushed into waiting boats.

Dear Ayesha,

In the **English** dictionary, the word **Holocaus**t, which has its origin in Hebrew, refers mainly to some 6 million Jews who were systematically exterminated by Nazi Germany during World War II, and it is described as 'one of the most horrific war crimes ever' in history. This was the 20th century; and the location was Nazi Germany and German-occupied Europe.

Up till the time of writing you this letter, Ayesha, this other **holocaust,** systematically committed over a period between the 15th and 19th centuries on African soil has not yet been identified by European historians.

About 15 million people were forced to migrate from Africa to the Western Hemisphere. More than 4million Africans died from the chains and beatings they received at the hands of slave traders walking through bushes, forests and valleys; Africans died in the forts and castles which housed the governors and officials of the conquering powers; and more Africans are yet to be accounted for in the journey ahead.

But read on.

At the Elmina Castle, a plaque next to the condemned cell reads:

"IN EVERLASTING MEMORY OF THE ANGUISH OF OUR ANCESTORS. MAY THOSE WHO DIED REST IN PEACE. MAY THOSE WHO RETURN FIND THEIR ROOTS. MAY HUMANITY NEVER AGAIN PERPETUATE SUCH INJUSTICE AGAINST HUMANITY. WE, THE LIVING, VOW TO UPHOLD THIS".

The words were composed and posted by the Chiefs of the area during the atonement ceremony that started off the Pan African Historical Theatre Festival (PANAFEST) in 1992.

Door of No Return now open

Dear Ayesha,

I will want you to remember these words from Maya Angelou's poem, **Still I rise**:

"Out of the huts of history's shame
I rise
Up from a past that's rooted in pain
I rise
I'm a black ocean, leaping and wide,
Welling and swelling I bear in the tide.
Leaving behind nights of terror and fear
I rise
Into a daybreak that's wondrously clear
I rise
Bringing the gifts that my ancestors gave,
I am the dream and the hope of the slave.
I rise.'

With Love,

Efo Kojo

Cape Coast Castle

Chapter 6

HELL ON THE SEAS

'Europe became the center of a world-wide system and it was European capitalism which set slavery and the Atlantic slave trade in motion' – Walter Rodney, *How Europe underdeveloped Africa*

'Slavery, (as argued by the slave masters in Deep South), was the foundation for a biblically sanctioned social system superior to that of the free states' – Colin Woodard, *American Nations: A History of the Eleven Rival Regional Cultures of North America.*

My Dear Ayesha,

Historians and researchers continue to figure out the specific numbers of Africans taken out of the continent, but it is known that Angola, Mozambique, Madagascar, Senegal, Gambia, Guinea Bissau, Guinea, Sierra Leone, Liberia, Cote d'Ivoire, Gold Coast (Ghana), Togo, Benin, Nigeria, Cameroon, Equatorial Guinea, Gabon, Republic of Congo, Democratic Republic of Congo provided the millions of manpower that crossed the seas to the other side to build economies and nations.

Joseph Inikori (1992) publishes in his book, **The Atlantic Slave Trade: Effects on Economies, Societies and Peoples in Africa**, that 8 million were forced out of Eastern Africa alone to be sent to Asia.

Dear Ayesha,

I would like you to get a few terminologies right. When historians talk about the Trans-Atlantic Slave Trade, they are talking about the selling of Africans as slaves across the Atlantic Ocean between Europe and the Americas.

The term Triangular Trade is also used in books. It also refers to three sides of the transatlantic slave trade: some ships took off from Europe to Africa, then to the Caribbean and the Americas, and back to Europe.

The situation where ships sailed directly from Africa with captives to either the Americas, North and South, or to the Caribbean Islands is referred to as the Middle Passage.

Dear Ayesha,

Just imagine that in spite of the treatment given to slaves in the dungeons, and through the tunnels, the suffering was not over.

Available researched documentation recounts that most slave ships had a captain and sometimes a surgeon on board. Reason is simple: the captain had the responsibility to discipline the inmates, and the surgeon was to ensure that the slaves were fit to go and work.

Slaves were first stripped naked for inspection of their bodies from head to toe by the doctor. And to ensure slaves did not escape, the captain and his assistants put them in chains, irrespective of age or gender.

The men were normally packed together and secured by leg irons. Because the space was so cramped, male captives were forced to crouch or lie down for the long journey. While men were kept below the deck, women and children were allowed limited freedom on deck, exposing the women to sexual abuse and violence by the crew members.

Dear Ayesha,

To ensure good health, the captain and surgeon allowed two meals a day for the passengers; those who refused to eat were forced to do so.

This, however, did not guarantee safety and comfort, if there was anything like that; diseases and strange illnesses took a toll on those who could not be helped by the doctor. Suffocation conditions gave rise to epidemics of fever and dysentery. Of course, any captive who died was thrown overboard.

The situation of overcrowding and insanitary conditions led some European governments, principally French and British, to introduce laws that reduced the numbers allowed on board, of course the interest being for the slaves to survive the hardships until the ultimate destination.

Dear Ayesha,

Africans, no matter which part of the continent they came from, did not just follow these European masters without complaining. Like they did in the forts and castles, they fought back against the indignities and humiliation. Some died; some were thrown overboard into the sea.

Research by former Director of the Wilberforce Institute for the Study of Slavery and Emancipation, Professor David Richardson and Dr David Eltis (2010) shows that there were 485 acts of **violent** resistance by Africans against slave ships and crews.

Out of the 392 insurrections by enslaved Africans recorded by Richardson, 90 per cent took place between 1698 and 1807. More than 360 ships experienced insurrection, 22 of which were planned by the Africans, and the rest instances of rebellion.

In one instance, recorded in the Boston Weekly Newsletter of April 1737, Captain Japhet Bird reports : "I thought all our troubles of this voyage were over; but on the contrary…on the 14th March, 1737…to our great amazement, about 100 men jumped overboard, most were recovered, … we lost three good men slaves who would not try to save themselves, but resolved to die and sunk directly down."

Yes, there were many like these men who chose death rather than enslavement.

Dear Ayesha,

I want you to read below portions of transcripts of two different accounts of life on board a slave ship as published in John Newton's Journal 1829.

The first is by Reverend Robert Walsh who had been assigned with others to intercept slave ships during the Anti-slavery campaigns, and the second is by a former enslaved African Olaudah Equiano.

Dear Ayesha,

Listen to Reverend Robert Walsh as he tells what he saw on a slave ship:

'The first object that struck us was an enormous gun, turning a swivel, on deck – the constant appendage of a pirate; and the next were large kettles for cooking, on the bows – the usual apparatus of a slaver. Our boat was now hoisted out and I went on board with the officers. When we mounted her decks, we found her full of slaves.

She had taken in, on the coast of Africa, 336 males and 226 females, making in all 562, and had been out seventeen days, during which she had thrown overboard 55. The slaves were all enclosed under grated hatchways between decks.

The space was so low that they sat between each other's legs and were stowed so close together that there was no possibility of their lying down or at all changing their position by night or day.

As they belonged to and were shipped on account of different individuals, they were all branded like sheep with the owner's marks of different forms. These were impressed under their breasts or on their arms, and as the mate informed me with perfect indifference 'burnt with the red hot iron'.

Over the hatchway stood a ferocious-looking fellow with a scourge of many twisted thongs in his hand, who was the slave driver of the ship, and whenever he heard the slightest noise below, he shook it over them and seemed eager to exercise it.

I was quite pleased to take this hateful badge out of his hand, and I have kept it ever since as a horrid memorial of reality, should I ever be disposed to forget the scene I witnessed."

Inhumanity and horror.
Credit:dailymail.co.uk

My dear Ayesha,

Now, listen to this other piece by Reverend Robert Walsh:

"The circumstances which struck me most forcibly was how it was possible for such a number of human beings to exist, packed up and wedged together as tight as they could cram, in low cells three feet high, the greater part of which, except that immediately under the grated hatchways, was shut out from light or air, and this when the thermometer, exposed to the open sky, was standing on our deck at 89 degrees.

The space between decks was divided into two compartments 3 feet by 18 and of the other 40 by 21; into the first were crammed the women and girls, into the second the men and boys: 226 fellow creatures were thus thrust into one space 288 feet square and 336 into another 800 feet square, giving to the whole an average of 2.3 inches and to each of the women not more than 13 inches".

Dear Ayesha,

Is the next piece familiar?

"The heat of these horrid places was so great and the odor so offensive that it was quite impossible to enter them".

And now this:

"On looking into the places where they were crammed, there were found some children next the sides of the ship, at the places most remote from light and air; they were lying nearly in a torpid state… the little creatures seemed indifferent to life or death".

Yes, I can understand how Reverend Robert Walsh feels:

"While expressing my horror at what I saw, I was informed by my friends, who had passed so long a time on the coast of Africa and visited so many ships, that this was the best they had seen."

Really?

Can you imagine one human being treating another like this ?

Dear Ayesha,

Olaudah Equiano was an enslaved African from Nigeria born in 1745. He came from an Igbo background where his villagers lived the communal life. His parents were farmers and he remembered that his family worked together on the farms growing yams and other foodstuffs in addition to cultivating tobacco and cotton.

In his village, there were blacksmiths who made weapons and other craftsmen made jewelry. Coming from a traditional African home, he had learnt that dead people received adequate attention and were kept securely in designated places where they would not lose the spiritual connection with the living. Spirits of the dead were not allowed to wonder aimlessly.

Olaudah witnessed humiliation in its severest form when he was brought on the slave ship. For the first time in his wildest dreams, let alone in his own eyes, he saw men, women and children strapped in a neck yolk as they stumbled towards the coast.

He saw imprisonment of slaves who rebelled for as long as eight months until the ship arrived at its destination. He saw human beings stripped to their waist, examined by the captain, haggled over and given an identification mark on their back.

In one case, he saw blood oozing out of the spots where the human beings were branded.

When it got to his turn, Olaudah fainted and was given First Aid. When he came round, he was offered food; he refused it. He was then tied to the windlass and flogged.

Dear Ayesha,

Olaudah was one of those who had been told they were being taken away to work in the white man's land. He was not one of those who after a few miles on the sea believed that they were going to be eaten.

In utter despair, though he couldn't swim, he threw himself over the side of the ship, only to be rescued by a netting which prevented precious commodities like him from committing suicide.

Next, Olaudah was transferred to the lower deck where slaves were shackled and manacled. He was made to lie wedged in such close quarters that he had scarcely room to turn himself.

His living space was about three square feet, hardly more than that of a corpse in its coffin. The air was noxious, and the constant rubbing of his chains raised sores on his wrists and ankles.

Dear Ayesha,

As the ship sailed on, as the true story unfolds, the full enormity of what was happening to him struck home, as it must have done to millions of other Africans.

Because of bad weather, the slaves stayed locked below in their chains for days at a time. The heat was suffocating, the stench unbearable.

Covered in sweat, vomit, and blood, the packed slaves created a miasma which rose through the gratings of the upper deck in a loathsome mist.

Olaudah recalls in his statement to the Anti-slavery movement, "the necessary tubs, full of excrement, almost suffocated us".

The shrieks of terrified slaves, conscious of the troubled spirits of the dead, mingled with the groans of the dying.

Dear Ayesha,

It was rare for a slave transport across the Atlantic not to give plenty of sustenance to the sharks swimming nearby.

Olaudah became sick and 'hoped to put an end to my miseries".

He envied the dead who were thrown overboard, believing that their spirits lived on, liberated from their shackles.

With time, his own spirits improved with the weather.

Captives on board slave ship

Dear Ayesha,

The slaves were usually allowed on deck twice a day, in chains. But, Olaudah, being a child of 12, went unfettered, and because he was sickly he was allowed more time on deck, where women slaves washed him and looked after him.

One day, Olaudah saw three slaves elude the netting and jump overboard. A boat was lowered, and to the anger of the captain, two of them succeeded in drowning. The third was brought back on deck and flogged viciously.

When at last, they sighted landfall the crew overjoyed, while the captives remained sullen and silent.

The story goes on to say that Olaudah was luckier than some.

His forcible separation from his beloved sister had occurred on the quay before he was taken to the slave ship.

But many families were now separated in the dockyard, and the air was filled with their shrieks and bitter lamentations.

They were lined up in rows, and at the sound of a drum-roll, buyers scrambled to pick out the slaves.

Dear Ayesha,

One of the most shocking discoveries of the 21st century is a 'Slave Bible" that was used during the slave trade. It is found in the Museum of the Bible in Washington DC, USA. This is the Bible that was used by Slave Masters during the most horrific inhuman trade in human beings ever recorded in history.

Anthony Schmidt, Associate Curator of Bible and Religion in America, told CBN News in February 2018 that parts of this bible were deleted to manipulate slaves in the early 1800s.

Fourteen out of 66 books are missing from this version of the Bible. "It starts off with the creation story…then it jumps to Joseph getting sold into slavery by his brothers and how that ends up being a good thing for him", says Dr Schmidt.

"We skip over the Israelites in slavery in Egypt being let out", says the curator.

In this Slave Bible, **references to freedom are omitted**.

Rather, the Bible highlights themes of being submissive; and the same thing goes on in the New Testament.

Listen to this explanation, Ayesha:

"The whole book of Revelations is left out, so there is no new Kingdom, no new world, nothing to look forward to", says Dr Schmidt.

What this means is that there was no hope for African slaves and they should not look forward to any such hope. Of course, it was easy for slave owners to just say they were good Christians and that they taught their slaves about God.

They could easily quote from the same Bible from favorite texts from both the Old and the New Testament to support their position.

The King James Bible Genesis Chapter IX, versus 18 to 27 was very convenient:

"And the sons of Noah that went forth from the ark were Shem, Ham, and Japheth: and Ham is the father of Canaan. These are the

three sons of Noah: and of them was the whole world overspread. And Noah began to be an husbandman, and he planted a vineyard: and he drank of the wine, and was drunken; and he was uncovered within his tent. And Ham, the father of Canaan, saw the nakedness of his father, and told his two brethren without. And Shem and Japheth took a garment, and laid it upon both their shoulders, and went backward, and covered the nakedness of their father; and their faces were backward, and they saw not their father's nakedness. And Noah awoke from his wine, and knew what his younger son had done unto him. And he said, Cursed be Canaan; a servant of servants shall he be unto his brethren.

And he said, Blessed be the Lord God of Shem; and Canaan shall be his servant. God shall enlarge Japheth, and he shall dwell in the tents of Shem;

and Canaan shall be his servant. And Noah lived after the flood three hundred and fifty years."

'Slave Bible' available at the Bible Museum in Washington, DC

Dear Ayesha,

Canaan was cursed because his father saw the nakedness of Noah and didn't cover him. His punishment was to be a servant's servant. Why didn't Noah punish or curse Ham?

Yet, in another boiled down, popular version, there is inserted 'The curse of Ham' and Canaan was dropped from the story. Ham was referred to as a black person and all his descendants were made Africans. Hence, all Africans are to be servants all their lives.

My dear Ayesha,

Now it is becoming clear that the Bible has been subject to various translations and interpretations that would justify whatever the writers or owners wanted to pursue.

Dear Ayesha,

So now, it is not just that there was a special edition of the Bible for Slave Masters, even those who used the regular Bible used specific interpretations to justify slavery.

Look at Apostle Paul's Epistle to the Ephesians, Chapter VI, versus 5-7:

"Servants, be obedient to them that are your masters according to the flesh, with fear and trembling, in singleness of your heart, as unto Christ; not with eye-service, as men-pleasers; but as the servants of Christ, doing the will of God from the heart; with good will doing service, as to the Lord, and not to men: knowing that whatsoever good thing any man doeth, the same shall he receive of the Lord, whether he be bond or free."

(Paul repeated himself, almost word for word, in the third chapter of his Epistle to the Colossians.)

This is what was drummed into the minds and hearts of all Africans that were converted, and this has continued till today.

Certain people referred to as 'Men of God' or simply 'White men' are looked upon with *fear and trembling;* everything they say is gospel truth and they cannot be questioned. This is part of the source for ensuring ***white supremacy***.

The fear of raising any questions against anybody who holds the Bible in most parts of Africa, and even in the diaspora, has contributed to the uncontrolled growth of charlatans exploiting masses of the populations.

Of course, this does not mean that other white or religious people did not oppose the slave trade; there were evangelicals and other anti-slavery campaigners who had other moral reasons to oppose the slave trade.

The Bible was used to protect the castles, canons and the trade therein

Dear Ayesha,

Different versions of the Bible also gave cause for pro-slavery campaigners to feel justified in their actions. One section that was also referred to is Leveticus Chapter 25, versus 44-45.

The **King James Version** reads:

"Both thy bondmen, and thy bondmaids, which thou shalt have, shall be of the heathen that are round about you; of them shall ye buy bondmen and bondmaids.

[45] *Moreover of the **children of the strangers that do sojourn among you**, of them shall ye buy, and of their families that are with you, which they begat in your land: and **they shall be your possession**.*

*[46] And ye shall take them **as an inheritance** for your children after you, to inherit them for a possession; **they shall be your bondmen for ever**: but over your brethren the children of Israel, ye shall not rule one over another with rigour.".*

The **New International Version** (NIV) also reads:

*[44] " 'Your **male and female slaves** are to come from the nations around you; from them you may buy slaves. [45] You may also buy some of the temporary residents living among you and members of their clans born in your country, and **they will become your property**. [46] You can bequeath them to your children as inherited property and can make them slaves for life, but you must not rule over your fellow Israelites ruthlessly."*

Dear Ayesha,

We are talking of times when European explorers granted charter by the King, also Head of the Church, considered the Bible as **infallible.** They believed every word with all their heart and therefore they knew what they were doing was in accordance with the word of God.

On the continent of Africa, we later saw the use of the Bible in justifying **Apartheid** in South Africa.

Dear Ayesha,

There is an interesting discussion among Bible scholars about the use of the term heathens, sometimes Gentiles, or sinners as referring to Africans. But pushed to a corner, some scholars say Africans knew Christianity as far back as the 2nd century AD in ancient Egypt and therefore could not be discriminated against in the Bible.

But again, that can raise further questions about who wrote the Bible, who translated it, and who interpreted it to suit what purpose.

But that discussion will continue for a long time.

Whichever way one saw it, Europeans had to have an excuse to drag Africans from the continent to use as slaves in their new periods of economic reconstruction. Religion was certainly used to advantage.

Dear Ayesha,

Listen to Martin Luther King:

"Three hundred years of humiliation, abuse and deprivation cannot be expected to find voice in a whisper."

And this one:

'To love someone who does not love you, is like shaking a tree to make the dew drops fall.' ~ African Proverb from The Congo

And here is Edmund Burke:

"Death is natural to a man, but slavery unnatural; and the moment you strip a man of his liberty you strip him of all his virtues: you convert his heart into a dark hole, in which all the vices conspire against you".

I will be back, Ayesha.

Efo Kojo

Chapter 7

BATTLING FOR DIGNITY

You cannot climb to the mountain top without crushing some weeds with your feet ~ African Proverb

A bridge is repaired only when someone falls into the water. ~ African Proverb

My dear Ayesha,

Our people have come a long way from Jamestown in Africa.

It has been a very long journey.

They have come from various parts of the continent.

They have been separated from their families, their cultures and their green environment.

They have been forced to abandon their farms, their crafts, their communal games, their loved ones.

Teiko, Akwele, Olaudah, Mutesa, Karimu, Miguel, Isabel, Rui, Kwame, Yaa, have all survived the arduous battle with inhumanity and have arrived in a foreign land.

Mind you, they sang songs – songs of hope, war songs – on the ships. Their melodious voices were unmistakable.

Occasionally they were flogged for making excessive noise and chanting inaudible words. In no time, all their names were changed into easily pronounceable ones. Teiko became Turner. Akwele became Anna. Olaudah was renamed Solomon. Mutesa was renamed Moses; Karimu was named Samuel; Miguel became Michael, Isabel changed to Isabella, Rui was given Robert, Kwame became Jacob, and Yaa was renamed Rebecca. In no logical order.

But the Africans persevered. They sparingly used their karaoke martial arts skills; yet they knew they had a weapon. They used any available piece of iron or steel to make drum music. Sometimes the slave master who enjoyed the rhythm took a step or two and ordered the female slaves to dance.

Three months on unfamiliar seas, losing mates and relations, watching others jump the ships to their death, witnessing suicide happen in the open, with occasional alert to listen to portions of the Bible being read by the captain.

Occasions came when ship captains and crew openly raped women and young girls. Yes, all these happened to satisfy somebody's greed:

To help grow an economy and build prosperity for others.

They twisted and erased the good news in the Bible.

And ensured that the news only favored a superior race.

Dear Ayesha,

There is no piece of evidence to show that potential and real slave owners in Virginia, South Carolina, North Carolina, Jamaica, Barbados, and elsewhere were a charitable breed of people ready to shower praises on this human cargo dumped on their shores.

What is known is that another round of sales was waiting for the Africans. On the deck of the ship, these Africans were paraded to be sold.

Tobacco planters lined up to select qualified candidates, negotiated for them and bought them. Remember the Bible verse? They were now **property** to be counted among the tobacco fields owned by the Masters. One by one, they were taken in different directions to the farms of their owners.

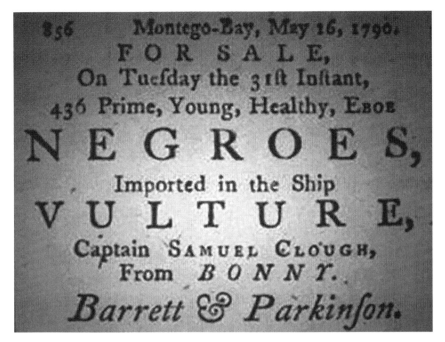

Slave sales notice

But wait a minute: the new environment did not suit all the newcomers.

In Virginia, some of them could not stand the new weather. New climate, strange diseases, unfriendly hosts. Some died in the first year.

It is also recorded that not all black Virginians were 'property' slaves. A few black people were allowed their freedom as 'indentured slaves' and they worked on farms and even owned servants. Yet the large majority had to endure their chattel slave status.

Dear Ayesha,

Whether captives were brought into Virginia or the West Indies by Portuguese, Dutch or British ships, treatment of slaves was no different.

Impoverished English immigrants were brought in as workers in Virginia after the massacre of the Powhatan Indians, but this did not change the status of the Africans.

The labor-intensive nature of the tobacco economy in Virginia by the 1660s depended more on African slaves, and the Royal African Company charted by the English government brought in more slaves through their business agents in Jamestown.

Dear Ayesha,

Get this right: Africans were not quiet, obedient and docile. They kicked, shouted, sang, jeered and became uncontrollable. They resisted and rebelled in many places across America and the Caribbean!

Africa and the Americas have their own local heroes. In his book **Abolition**! Richard S. Reddie lists men and women such as Nzinga Mbemba of the Congo, King Agaja of Dahomey, Nanny and Cudjoe in Jamaica, Cuffy and Quamina Gladstone in Guyana and <u>Bussa</u> in Barbados.

There are several recorded cases of rebellion, but I will narrate just a few.

In **Barbados**, a number of small-scale insurrections were reported between1629 and 1701, but when it appeared that slaves had been subdued, something happened on Easter Sunday April 14, 1816.

Earlier in 1815, the Barbadian House of Assembly had discussed the Imperial Registry Bill which aimed at registering all colonial slaves. An enslaved African named *Bussa,* then began organizing slaves on various plantations to begin discussing and protesting the bill before it became law.

Joined by other slaves and domestic servants, principally *John* and *Nanny Grigg, Bussa* led the rebellion to overthrow their masters and gain their freedom. The entire island got shaken as thousands of slaves picked up their tools and began chasing their masters and setting their farms on fire.

About 70 estates, more than a quarter of the island's sugar cane plantation, went up in flames.

Dear Ayesha,

The response of the infuriated masters was quick and expected: martial law was declared. The imperial guards and the local militia went into action and slaughtered about 1000 Africans.

Another 214, including Bussa were executed in public, and 123 were sold and transferred to other plantations in British colonies in the neighborhood.

A white Barbadian sent this letter to London:

"The disposition of the enslaved persons in general is very bad. They are sullen and sulky and seem to cherish feelings of deep revenge. We hold the West Indies by a very precarious tenure – that of military strength only. I would not give a year's purchase for any island we now have".

Dear Ayesha,

Jamaica had series of revolts, with not less than 20 recorded between 1655 and 1813. Over 2,500 Africans are said to have escaped from the plantations. Uprisings and mutinies were regular between 1816 and 1823.

'Tacky's Rebellion' of 1760 took six months to put down. But there is one major rebellion, also named the Great Slave revolt of 1831 which shook the Caribbean world and which has attracted many historians and researchers.

Led by Samuel Sharpe, African slaves declared a strike action to ask their masters to pay them for their work. When their demands fell on deaf ears, 20,000 Africans seized over 200 plantations and burnt down houses and warehouses containing sugar cane belonging to their white masters, amounting to over one million pounds.

The 10-day rebellion destabilized Jamaica for over one month, after which it was quelled by British troops. 750 Africans were convicted out of the hundreds arrested, and 138 were sentenced to death.

Events in the same year elsewhere showed clearly that it was not just in Jamaica that Africans were rebelling. But it was significant that only a week after the execution of Samuel Sharpe, the British Parliament appointed a committee to consider actively listening to the demand for freedom by the slaves.

Dear Ayesha,

I cannot tell you about slave rebellion in Jamaica without mentioning this Ashanti female slave who grew to become a national hero.

Known variously as Granny **Nanny** or just Nanny, she is known to have successfully organized guerilla warfare during the 18th century to keep away the British troops who attempted to attack them in the mountains. She was an escaped slave from the Ashanti ethnic group and shipped from present-day Ghana.

Queen Nanny of Jamaica

She is said to have possessed supernatural and magical powers and became the icon of the maroons of Jamaica who still practice many aspects of Ashanti culture.

Nanny has been described as a practitioner of Obeah, a term used in the Caribbean to describe a folk belief system based on African powerful influences. Obeah, later to be outlawed by the colonial authorities for being 'evil and fetish', aided the Africans as a source of strength and resistance.

The Obeah woman like Nanny, was regarded as a community leader and teacher of African folk cultural heritage. She was highly respected and feared by all who met her for possessing supernatural powers.

Some historians believe that Obeah came to the Caribbean from Kromantse (Coromantine) in the central region of modern Ghana.

My dear Ayesha,

In Georgetown, **Guyana**, stands the Monument of 'Cuffy' to commemorate the Revolution of February 23, 1763. Cuffy, or Kofi of Gold Coast (now Ghana) origin, led 2,500 slaves including Atta, Assabre, and Akara, to revolt against harsh treatment and brutal punishments by their masters.

Monument of Cuffy (Kofi Badu) in Georgetown, Guyana

Dear Ayesha,

The modern-day country of **Haiti** had in a lot of ways inspired what the British government experienced in its colonies.

Then called Saint Domingue, this rich colony was controlled by the French. Slaves were taught a new language Creole, and a new religion voudou evolved out of their traditional practices and Christianity. The colony had the most prosperous sugar industry, thanks to the hard work of enslaved Africans who were forced out of the continent. Saint Domingue boasted as the world's single largest producer of sugar and coffee, all on the back of over worked and underfed Africans under very harsh conditions.

One account had it that it was in Saint Domingue that slaves lived in windowless huts, were whipped regularly, and had salt, pepper and hot ashes poured onto their bleeding wounds. Yes, some plantation owners were not prepared to heed to the decree coming out of France for slaves to be granted some rights under the 'Declaration of the Rights of Man'.

The bells of Liberty, Equality and Fraternity were ringing out loud in France in the late 1780s, and common people were collapsing state power and the power of the ruling class.

Enslaved Africans, who had been resisting oppression all these years, decided in 1791 to turn the

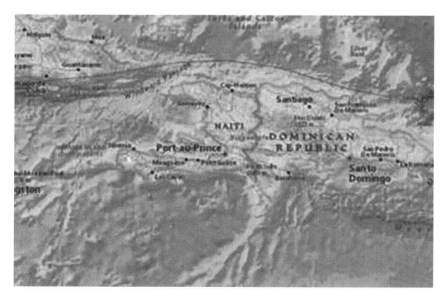

Haiti

tables on their masters. This time, led by Tousaint L'Ouverture, an African, they picked up machetes, hooks and torches and lit flames in sugar cane plantation warehouses, while killing their white masters.

Fire razed down hundreds of acres of sugar and coffee farms and hundreds of Europeans were murdered. This shocked the European world, naturally, as for the first time the rebels were determined to take over power in the colony. This was a bloody rebellion.

The rebels won: the agents of the French government abolished slavery in the colony in October 1793, and the National Convention in Paris endorsed it by eventually abolishing slavery throughout all its territories on 4th February,1794.

This happened in spite of the fact that the French-British War of 1793 had given the British hope that they were going to take over Saint Domingue. Afraid of Tousaint L'Ouverture and his revolutionary government, the British retreated.

Dear Ayesha,

European leaders never learnt their lessons. When Napoleon Bonaparte seized power in France in 1799, he issued a decree saying that the following words be inscribed in gold letters on all the flags of the battalions of the National Guard in Saint L'Ouverture:

"Remember, brave blacks, that the French people alone recognize your freedom and the equality of your rights".

This was regarded as a slap in the face of the fighting Africans.

L'Ouverture responded sharply:

"It is not a circumstantial freedom conceded to ourselves alone that we want. It is the absolute adoption of the principle that any man born red, black or white cannot be the property of his like. We are free today because we are the stronger party".

This angered Napoleon, and as history has it, in May of 1802 he restored slavery and the slave trade in France and its colonies, spurring new waves of violence in the Caribbean. He dispatched an army of 35,000, described as the largest invasion force ever to leave France, to Saint Domingue. Toussaint L'Ouverture was captured, but the French lost the war. Leaders of Saint Domingue proclaimed a free sovereign country and named it *Haiti*, after an original Indian name.

Dear Ayesha,

It is interesting to note that prior to the French Revolution, a former slave ship captain, Pruneau de Pommegorge, who commanded the French Royal ship in Dahomey in the late 1760s was moved to comment about the whole slavery and slave trade business.

He wrote in the book, *Description de la Negrete:*

'By what right do we permit ourselves to take men away from their homeland? To cause massacres and continual wars there? To separate mothers from their children, husbands from their wives? To cause those who are too old to be sold to be massacred in front of their children, because of our lust to buy these unfortunates?'

Revolts continued on other Caribbean islands such as Grenada, Saint Lucia and the Antilles during the same period 1789-1815.

Dear Ayesha,

The question is: what was happening on American soil itself?

The first recorded slave revolt is reported to have happened in 1663 as a joint operation between enslaved Africans and indentured white servants; but it was not until 1687 that an all-black revolt occurred in **Virginia**.

In 1739, one of the bloodiest slave rebellions started near the Stono River Bridge near Charleston, **South Carolina**.

The State historic marker narrates:

"The Stono Rebellion, the largest slave insurrection in British North America, began nearby on September 9, 1739. About 20 Africans raided a store near Wallace Creek, a branch of the Stono River. Taking guns and other weapons, they killed two shop keepers. The rebels marched south toward promised freedom in Spanish Florida, waving flags, beating drums and shouting 'Liberty !'.

The rebels were joined by 40 to 60 more during their 15-mile march. They killed at least 20 whites, but spared others. The rebellion ended late that afternoon when the militia caught the rebels, killing at least 34 of them. Most who escaped were captured and executed; any forced to join the rebels were released.

The South Carolina state assembly soon enacted a harsh slave code, in force until 1865."

Another extended version adds that

'Charleston had 19 years earlier been the center of a plotted revolt by 14 slaves planning to destroy plantations and attack Charleston. Betrayed, they fled, attempted to convince Creek Indians to join their uprising and were captured in Savannah, Georgia. All were executed upon return to Charleston'.

Dear Ayesha,

I think it is important to know that before the uprising, the white colonists were working on a **Negro Act** because they were not comfortable with the increasing number of blacks in the area.

The Negro Act limited the numbers and movement of blacks. The Act, which was finalized and approved soon after the Stono Rebellion, no longer allowed African slaves to grow their own food, assemble in groups and earn their own money.

There definitely was a cause for rebellion. Enslaved Africans needed to make choices to improve upon their conditions of living. They couldn't remain property of other people all their lives.

The news of slaves in Saint Domingue seizing on the egalitarian rhetoric of the American and French revolution in 1793 to overthrow their masters began to horrify whites in South Carolina. The unrest continued.

In 1816, in **Camden**, also in South Carolina, slaves planned to set fire to the houses of plantation and slave owners and kill the white population. The seventeen slaves arrested were jailed and seven were executed.

This did not stop another successful attempt being made in 1829 during which 85 houses of white masters were torched and razed to the ground.

Dear Ayesha,

Revolts were not happening only in the Southern parts of America.

New York City by the beginning of the 18th century had 20 percent of its population coming from the enslaved African warriors, particularly from the Gold Coast, now Ghana.

It is part of this group, armed with guns, swords, knives and axes, that planned an uprising in April 1712 with local Indians and set fire to a slave owner's home.

Robberies, arsons and revolts continued for a long time in Rhodes Island, Albany, and in New York city itself.

On what was known as the **German Coast,** enslaved Africans planned in 1811 to destroy sugar cane plantations, free every slave across the Mississippi River and take control of New Orleans. When their plans failed, the 40 out of 100 slaves who were captured were executed, and their corpses displayed in public as a deterrent to any future rebellions.

My dear Ayesha,

I would like you to study and memorize these great sayings and quotes:

'We have come over a way that with tears has been watered,
We have come, treading our path through the blood of the slaughtered.'

James Weldon Johnson, Lift Every Voice and Sing (Stanza 2)

'Every great dream begins with a dreamer. Always remember, you have within you the strength, the patience, and the passion to reach for the stars to change the world'. – Harriet Tubman

With Love,

Efo Kojo

The Negro Speaks of Rivers
(To W.E.B. DuBois)

I've known rivers:
I've known rivers ancient as the world and older than the flow
of human blood in human veins.

My soul has grown deep like the rivers.

I bathed in the Euphrates when dawns were young.
I built my hut near the Congo and it lulled me to sleep.
I looked upon the Nile and raised the pyramids above it.
I heard the singing of the Mississippi when Abe Lincoln went
down to New Orleans, and I've seen its muddy bosom
turn all golden in the sunset.

I've known rivers:
Ancient, dusky rivers.

My soul has grown deep like the rivers.

(Poem by Langston Hughes)

Chapter 8

AN EXPLOSIVE REBELLION AND A CIVIL WAR

"In a world filled with hate, we must still dare to hope. In a world filled with anger, we must still dare to comfort. In a world filled with despair, we must still dare to dream. And in a world filled with distrust, we must still dare to believe." – Michael Jackson

"We got to fight the system, because God never made no difference between black, white, blue, pink or green. People is people" –Bob Marley

My dear Ayesha,

In August 1994, I was taken on a tour of the Nat Turner Trail in Virginia, USA, by Mr Khalif Khalifa, then Chief Executive of the publishing firm US&UB Books, based on the farm.

This is a huge 123-acre property originally owned by Benjamin Turner, believed to be the father of Nat Turner, in the Southampton County. I drove in Khalifa's jeep across 23 or more locations that were included in the path followed by Nat Turner and his army to stage probably the biggest rebellion in American history.

After nearly two hours, we ended up in a library, named after Nat Turner, to imbibe the full essence of the revolt.

I accepted a glass of fresh juice and listened anxiously to the story:

On Sunday August 21, 1831, at about noon, four African slaves - Henry, Hark, Nelson and Sam – met on a quiet part of a plantation owned by Joseph Travis to enjoy a barbecue. They brought in their own pig, brandy and plates. They were soon joined by two novices, Will and Jack.

After three hours, the main brain behind the barbecue arrived. He was a stout, heavily built African with dark complexion, his name Nat Turner. The plantation belonged to his master, Travis. He said 'hi' to everybody and took his seat.

While they chewed on the pork, Nat Turner laid out the plan: they were to pick up some guns belonging to their masters and, accompanied later in the night by more recruits, butcher slave owners on all 23 sites and win their freedom. He had been preaching to them so they understood him. The six others gave thumps up.

After two weeks chase round the plantations executing their plan, 50 white men, women, and children were killed before Turner's army was finally overcome.

According to my tour guide: *'What you saw is a retrace of the route that Nat Turner, a Chattel Slave whose persona was so dynamic, took and caused his fellow captives to overcome their fears of a cruel, demonic Slave master, to rise up and kill him, and others, free fellow slaves, and expropriate stolen property'.*

Khalifa continued, as I listened attentively:

'The Nat Turner Trail is a visit to the battle sites where he fought against slave owners, while making his way to Jerusalem. After Nat Turner, the name Jerusalem was changed to Courtland. Courtland today, as was Jerusalem, was the County Seat'.

Dear Ayesha,

Nat Turner must have been a very brave person from the kind of insights I picked even from his own confessions narrated to his lawyer before his execution.

Without a doubt he was dealing a heroic blow to a very unjust and repressive system, and his goal to end the institution of slavery must have overshadowed any risks and even morals that attended his action.

I bought myself a copy of the *Confessions of Nat Turner* which was on sale. Turner's own words, even as I read again today, are as graphic and chilling as they must have been in 1831, the same year in which rebellions and uprisings were becoming rife in the plantations in British West Indies.

Dear Ayesha,

Turner was a Christian, grown to become a Baptist Minister, mind you. He was a preacher who had been ministering to some of his own slave mates. As he himself says in his confessions:

"Knowing the influence I had obtained over the minds of my fellow-servants...by the communion of the Spirit, whose revelations I often communicated to them... I now began to prepare them for my purpose."

Turner claimed that though he had been well treated by his master, he had been seeing visions, voices and signals from God including 'a bluish color visible in the sun a week prior to the revolt and a solar eclipse earlier in the year'.

He was willing to shed the first blood of his own master and that of his family:

'It was then observed that I must spill the first blood. On which, armed with a hatchet, and accompanied by Will, I entered my master's chamber, it being dark, I could not give a death blow; the hatchet glanced from his head, he sprang from the bed and called his wife, it was his last word. Will laid him dead, with a blow of his axe, and Mrs. Travis shared the same fate, as she lay in bed.'(Confession of Nat Turner)

Certainly, this must have been a tough decision to make, but, as my tour guide concluded, *'this was one grand, gallant attempt to free every Black man, woman and child from chattel slavery, second-class citizenship and other forms of oppression'*.

According to Turner's own confession, he was betrayed by two slaves who had stumbled on his hiding place. He was caught 'under the top of a fallen tree' and the following day Nat Turner "confessed" to his court-appointed attorney, Thomas Gray.

At his trial on November 5, 1831, Nat Turner was sentenced to die by hanging for his role in the slave rebellion. On November 11, 1831, Nat Turner was publicly hung.

Dear Ayesha,

Discussions about Nat Turner still continue among historians and commentators, but you will understand from all the stories

I have told you that he was prepared to sacrifice himself for the black race.

Here was a self-educated Christian who believed that there was a Day of Judgement. Did the Christianity that had enveloped him have any messianic overtones that he alone could decipher? Did other slaves believe in him because they were expecting a divine intervention to deliver them from the unjust social order and punish their oppressors?

Dear Ayesha,

It is important to analyze Nat Turner in greater depth because his background differs from that of other rebel leaders we have come across so far.

Here was an educated minister as well as a slave. Rare combination, isn't it?

Turner told attorney Thomas Ruffin Gray in *"The Confessions of Nat Turner"* that when he was three or four years old, he could provide details of events that occurred before his birth. His astonished mother and others took the comments as signs that he was a prophet and "intended for some great purpose."

The young slave showed "uncommon intelligence" and was taught to read and write. His deeply religious grandmother nurtured his spiritual development. *"To a mind like mine, restless, inquisitive and observant of everything that was passing, it is easy to suppose that religion was the subject to which it would be directed,"* said Turner. And he says that he regularly read the Bible and preached to his fellow slaves.

Again, Dear Ayesha,

Turner says that when he was 21, he followed in his father's footsteps and escaped from his owner. To the astonishment of his fellow slaves, however, the future rebel leader came back to the plantation after spending 30 days in the woods because, as Turner reportedly told Gray, *"the Spirit appeared to me and said I had my wishes directed to the things of this world, and not to the kingdom of heaven, and that I should return to the service of my earthly master."* Elsewhere, Turner would be taken to a superior priest for 'further prayers' for these unusual revelations.

Turner had other revelations: he confessed to Gray that he received *divine visions to avenge slavery and lead his fellow slaves from bondage.*

The most vivid of these visions came on May 12, 1828, when Turner *"heard a loud noise in the heavens, and the Spirit instantly appeared to me and said the serpent was loosened, and Christ had laid down the yoke he had borne for the sins of men, and that I should take it on and fight against the serpent, for the time was fast approaching when the first should be last and the last should be first."*

Clearly this was a divine call which he could not disobey.

Dear Ayesha,

As an African from the continent, I can relate to the kinds of vision Turner had, very similar to some of the revelations pronounced in 'spiritual' churches. He saw an eruption of Mount St. Helens as the signal to launch the rebellion, linking it to a solar eclipse that had occurred on February 12, 1831.

The spiritual connotations of what Turner 'confessed' will be of interest for a very long while.

Dear Ayesha,

The effect of the action by Nat Turner and his Black Liberation Army, as is called, cannot be underestimated.

It is reported that in the wake of the Turner-led Rebellion, some States passed laws making it illegal to *teach African Americans how to read and write*. It was a catalyst to the radicalization of American politics.

As one historian puts it, the rebellion 'marked the end of a nascent abolitionist movement'. The Legislature in Virginia rejected narrowly a motion for gradual emancipation of blacks, to follow the lead of the North.

So, what was happening elsewhere?

My dear Ayesha,

Rebellion was in the air. Those enslaved were struggling to free themselves from bondage. Those who wanted to maintain their supremacy were in no mood to allow freedom for others.

Meanwhile, slave ship revolts continued.

There was this Spanish ship called **Amistad.** It was shipping enslaved Africans out of Cuba to another location. Luck was not on the side of the captains. This was in 1839. 53 Africans seized control of the vessel and asked two officers to take them back to Africa.

The ship wandered the seas for two months not knowing what to do. It eventually docked in Long Island, and the Africans were captured. The Africans did not give up. They fought their case in court for nearly two years, after which they were deported back to West Africa.

Dear Ayesha,

On another side of America, the ship **Creole** was also leaving Richmond to go to New Orleans to sell a cargo of tobacco and 135 slaves in November 1841. The slaves, sensing the motives of the captain on board, unanimously agreed to rebel. They seized control of the ship and succeeded in diverting their journey to the Bahamas. They got their freedom.

Did anybody suspect a civil war was in the offing in America? Maybe Yes, maybe No.

In 1859 alone, several armed slave uprisings were reported in Mississippi, West Virginia, Missouri, Kentucky and North Carolina.

The following year 1860, arson and slave rebellions shook Alabama, Texas, Georgia, North Carolina and other Southern States. A total number of 14 cities in north Texas were also affected.

Dear Ayesha,

Very few Africans on the continent know that the civil war people talk about in America was over the African slaves. On the continent of Africa, civil wars are fought over land, mineral resources, greed, and sometimes petty nationalism.

In America, when Abraham Lincoln was elected in 1860 as President of the United States, there were those in the Southern states who favored having and expanding control over slaves against in the those in the North who wanted a level of freedom for these Africans.

Seven Southern states formed themselves into the Confederate States of America – South Carolina, Mississippi, Florida, Alabama, Georgia, Louisiana, and Texas - and decided to secede from the rest in the Union.

So, Southern nationalism against Northern nationalism? All over morality over the issue of African slaves? This should be a topic for discussion by African leaders. Funny?

Dear Ayesha,

April 12, 1861 comes.

Confederate forces attack a major US fortress, Fort Sumter, in the harbor of Charleston, South Carolina; the Union would resist it and a war starts.

History carries on from here till Emancipation in 1865 as the period for the Civil War.

But there are several reports which confirm that throughout the civil war in America, there were major instances of unrest, civil disobedience, uprisings and resistance among slaves in the southern states until the Confederate States were defeated.

The cost of the civil war in America? Some 620,000 soldiers killed, millions more injured, and a greater part of the South left in ruins. The manufacturing and industrial North retained its economic strength, with all the labor of blacks, as opposed to the large scale plantation-led agricultural economy of the South that also depended very heavily on the labor of African slaves.

Dear Ayesha,

Read my short poem:

The sweat, the toil, the sacrifices of our fathers,
The cries of our running and abandoned mothers,
The tears of sandwiched and motherless children,
The dispossession of language, drum and music,
The surrender to murder, defeacation and brutality,
The stony silence of human beings –
Did we have to endure all these?
For humankind, for human good, for freedom for all !

Dear Ayesha,

I hope you now understand the contribution that Africans have made to the building of the United States of America.

Remember these quotes:

"We are the heirs of a past of rope, fire and murder. I for one am not ashamed of this past. My shame is for those who became so inhuman that they could inflict torture on us". – Martin Luther King, Jr.

"If you have no confidence in self, you are twice defeated in the race of life" – Marcus Garvey.

Dear Ayesha,

Africans must be very proud of their heritage. In spite of all that Europeans, and now some Americans, did to spit on the African, dehumanize them, and tell them they were inferior, our people continued to resist!

The story continues!

Best wishes, Ayesha.

Efo Kojo

Chapter 9

THE DIVISION OF A CONTINENT

Greed, Invasion, Colonization, Occupation, Humiliation, Division......nothing more !

My dear Ayesha,
There is a book I was required to study for my first degree at the University of Ghana. The title was *'Heart of Darkness'* – by Joseph Conrad, a famous Polish-British writer. Several themes run through the story in which a businessman Kurtz settles in Congo with a 'heavenly mission' to spread the light of Christianity to civilize the natives out of 'darkness'. Marlow, a sailor, takes up a job with the trading company and discovers several aspects of imperialism. The book exposes the naked and dirty faces of exploitation, racial discrimination, colonialism and sheer cruelty of the European towards the African.

Though this book is fiction, one cannot fail to see a reflection of the thinking of those who conceived of Africa as 'property' in a dark continent, least of all King Leopold II of Belgium.

Dear Ayesha,
Before I say a little more about the Congo and King Leopold, let me tell you something else. We left off with a civil war in America fought over the morality or otherwise of slavery and

slave trade. After the war, those who argued for abolition of the inhuman trade got the upper hand, and America got united.

America suffered. Not just with the loss of lives, but even more important for the government, with the economy. After Emancipation came the reconstruction of a United States of America. Roads, telecommunication, education, housing, agriculture, health services – all these sectors needed money, particularly when their banks had crashed. The economy began to face difficulties.

But more difficulties were facing Europe which had overstretched itself and taken up various colonies in the Americas, West Indies, and were looking into Asia.

At the time, there was what was termed the "Economic Depression" experienced from the year 1873 and was continuing into the 1880s. Officially chattel slavery had been abolished in British territories in 1834, and in America in 1865; most countries' economies were crumbling.

In 1862, Prince Otto Edward Leopold von Bismarck, Prime Minister of Prussia, who hated democracy and socialism, began his crusade use force to unite all the small states around Prussia into a German Empire. Of course, he had upset the balance of power in Europe.

Dear Ayesha,

At that time, Africa was largely unexplored. Apart from the focused trade in slaves and other commodities, mainly taking place on the coasts, even maps around the continent were not common. Explorers like David Livingstone and H.M. Stanley were now charting the River Nile from its source, and tracing the courses of River Niger, Congo and the Zambezi. And that is how they found the vast natural and mineral resources of the continent of Africa. While de Brazza was exploring the Kongo Kingdom for France, Stanley also explored it in the early 1880s on behalf of King Léopold II of Belgium, who would have his personal Congo Free State. For Britain, Germany, France and Belgium whose economies were suffering, Africa was the opportunity.

Dear Ayesha,

Those were the days when Kingdoms of the Ashanti, Zulu, Moroccan, Abyssinia (later Ethiopia), reigned supreme and stood to resist European incursions into their kingdoms.

Dear Ayesha,

Meanwhile, Europeans were hungry for copper, cotton, rubber, palm oil, cocoa, diamonds, tea, and tin, to which European consumers had grown accustomed and upon which European industry had grown dependent. France occupied Tunisia in May 1881 and Guinea in 1884. The same year, Britain occupied Egypt, which ruled over Sudan, and parts of Chad, Eritrea, and Somalia. In 1870 and 1882, Italy took possession of the first parts of Eritrea, while Germany declared Togoland, the Cameroons and South West Africa to be under its protection in 1884. Two countries were free of colonial rule: Ethiopia, Liberia.

Dear Ayesha,

German Emperor King Otto Von Bismarck proposed and called for a meeting of European leaders in Berlin in 1884. His reason made public was : to come to agreement on ownership over Africa and prevent war among the superpowers. Yes, he was tired of going to war, but there was something more hidden. He made it clear that if superpowers did not sit down to agree on who occupied the various parts of this resource-rich African region, they would find themselves fighting each other. Again, it was necessary to ensure that nations who claimed ownership of any part of Africa actually occupied it.

Have you heard of King Leopold II? He was cousin of Queen Victoria of England. It was he who established an international charitable organization and told the world he was going to take care of the primitive Africans in the colony of Congo. Part of his business was what Joseph Conrad was talking about in *Heart of Darkness.* You know what he did ? He told the European leaders that he had a plan on how to colonize Africa, but his colony of the Congo, called the Free State, would not be part of the negotiations.

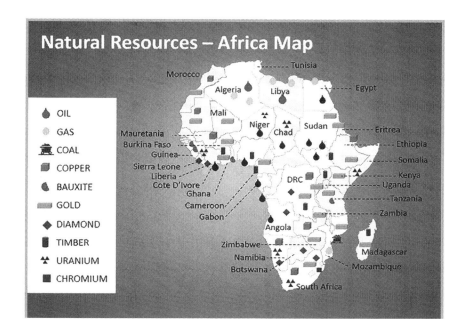

Natural Resources – Africa Map

Dear Ayesha,

Therefore, they drew their own boundaries.

At the end of the day, Britain took over Egypt and Anglo-Egyptian Sudan, Nigeria, Ghana, Sierra Leone, Gambia, British Somaliland, Rhodesia, Bechuanaland (South Africa). France won French West Africa, Tunisia, Morocco, Algeria, Madagascar, Gabon, and a slice of Somaliland. Belgium retained Belgian Congo. Portugal was allowed occupation of Angola, Mozambique. Italy was rewarded with Libya and a slice of Somaliland. Spain was given occupation of part of Morocco and Rio de Oro. Ethiopia (Abyssinia) and Liberia remained independent.

My dear Ayesha,

This explains where we are as a people on the continent of Africa. What will even make you understand why there are so many civil wars in Africa is the way ethnic groups were just shared like pieces of cake.

In East Africa, the Maasai were split between Kenya (62%) and Tanzania (38%). The Anyi (Akan) people were divided between Ghana (58%) and Cote d'Ivoire (42%). Mozambique was forced to share the Chewa tribe (50%) with Malawi (34%), and Zimbabwe (16%). And then the Malinkes (Mandinkas) also spread out across Gambia, Guinea, Sierra Leone, Liberia, Burkina Faso and other parts of West Africa.

The Ndembus are found in Angola, Zaire and Zambia. And the Nukwes are also split between Angola, Namibia, Botswana and Zambia. Researchers **Stelios Michalopoulos, Elias Papaioannou** observe aptly that 'civil conflict is concentrated in the historical homeland of partitioned ethnicities'. They note further that during the period 1970-2005, 'the groups with the highest incidence of civil war are the Afar and Esa', the Afar being partitioned between Ethiopia, Eritrea and Djibouti, and the Esa being split between Ethiopia and Somalia.

Dear Ayesha,

You must now be understanding why civil wars are more common in certain parts of the African continent than others. The European leaders must have known what they were doing: partitioning was a sure way of spurring civil conflict and unrest. And, mind you, where civil wars are common, there are mineral resources or strips of land at the center of the conflict.

Colonialism and its attendant imperialism, coming after the Berlin conference, brought in their wake a lot of impunity from white Europeans. Imagine that this British Government inspired imperialist called Cecil Rhodes, just like King Leopold of the Congo, acquired personal property over what is now Zimbabwe and named it after named after himself (Rhodesia).

In what is now Rwanda, German colonialism divided the local ethnic group in order to control them. They just took one social rich class and called them one ethnic group, and the rest another. The genocide we witnessed in 1994 was a direct consequence of this.

As for the French, they had a totally different form of domination. We learnt in school that it was called *assimilation.* It was like saying, we are stripping you of your dark color and identity and raise your status so you can be closer to the white French. You have better employment opportunities if you can speak French as good as the white person. As for the conditions for countries wanting total independence, we shall come to it later.

Dear Ayesha,

Trust Africans. They watched colonialists using *indirect rule* and various strategies to divide their people for a while before striking back. In East Africa, there was the Mau Mau Uprising of 1952-60 was led by Jomo Kenyatta; Zimbabwe's war of independence 1965-79 led by Robert Mugabe and others was a clear example. In the Portuguese colonies of Mozambique, Angola, Cape Verde and Guinea Bissau, struggles were waged before independence. The anti-apartheid revolts in South Africa are very well known. Unfortunately, attempts are being made today to label most of the leaders of the African revolts as dictators.

All the struggles waged on the continent against colonialism were intrinsically against white supremacy and restoration of the African identity. It is true that Africa did not have one identity as a continent before the infamous Scramble for the continent's resources, but what existed at the time was respect for our kingdoms and societies, with our cultural practices and values.

Dear Ayesha,

Read what African leaders said about the Scramble for Africa:

"They took our lands, our lives, our resources, and our dignity. Without exception, they left us nothing but our resentment, and later our determination to be free and rise once more to the level of man and woman who walk with their heads held high." Kwame Nkrumah (In "Africa Must Unite")

"When the Missionaries arrived, the Africans had the land and the Missionaries had the Bible. They taught how to pray with our eyes closed. When we opened them, they had the land and we had the Bible." — *Jomo Kenyatta (In "Facing Mount Kenya")*

Robert Mugabe: "We of Africa protest that, in this day and age, we should continue to be treated as lesser human beings than other races".

Robert Mugabe

Walter Rodney: "It was economics that determined that Europe should invest in Africa and control the continent's raw materials and labor. It was racism which confirmed the decision that the form of control should be direct colonial rule." (In "How Europe Underdeveloped Africa").

In May,1873, on his death bed, David Livingstone, the famous European explorer, who built the roadmap to Africa, called for a world-wide crusade to divide the continent. His motive:

Commerce, Christianity and Civilization, what he called the 3Cs.

Ayesha, there is more to learn. Don't stop learning.

Efo Kojo

Chapter 10

THE RALLYING CALL

(The rise of Pan-Africanism)

Marcus Garvey: ***The Black skin is not a badge of shame, but rather a glorious symbol of national greatness."***

My dear Ayesha,

We have come a long way. Out of the black skin have grown several pigmentations. Now we don't only have white skin; we have the yellow, the dark, the albino, the light-skinned, name them. Blacks never hated anybody with a different skin. At no time did people with black skin say they were superior. On the other hand, when invasion, conquest, slavery and occupation occurred, the presumption of superiority set in. And this presumption turned into a credo, an ideology and a faith, and blacks have become like the underdogs. But, as you have seen and read, it is wrong to think that blacks have accepted that position lying down. They have always resisted, and sometimes very violently.

At the end of the First World War, when the Constitution of America had endorsed equality of all races, and when strong European countries like Germany had also suffered defeat, and the Treaty of Versailles of 1919 was basing its raison d'etre on the ideal of self-determination, some eminent black leaders decided to act.

Dear Ayesha,

Prior to the end of the World War, a number of newspapers had sprung up in various parts of Africa to condemn colonialism. In Ghana alone, according to historian Adu Boahen, there were no less than 10 newspapers including the *Gold Coast Aborigines (1898),* the *Gold Coast Free Press (1899)* and *the Gold Coast Leader.* Nigeria had five newspapers including the *Lagos Standard (1895),* the *Lagos Weekly Record (1891),* the *Nigerian Chronicle (1908),* the *Nigerian Pioneer (1914), and the Nigerian Times (1910).* In Uganda, the *Ebifa Mu Uganda (1907)* was also founded to attack colonialism. Down South Africa, the *Imvozaba Ntsundu (Native Opinion)* was in circulation in 1915 in both English and Xhosa.

Dear Ayesha,

Let me add, that way back in 1906, a South African scholar and lawyer, from Natal, Isaka Seme, who along with other black activists founded the African Native National Congress, was addressing Royal African Society of London in the following words:

"The pyramids of Egypt are structures to which the world presents nothing comparable. These mighty monuments seem to look with disdain on very other work of human art and vie with nature herself. All the glory of Egypt belongs to Africa and her people. These monuments are the indestructible memorials of their great original genius. But it is not through Egypt alone that Africa claims such unrivalled historic achievements. I could have spoken of the pyramids of Ethiopia, which, though inferior in size to those in Egypt, far surpass them in architectural beauty; their sepulchers, which evince the highest purity of taste; and of many prehistoric ruins in other parts of Africa. In such ruins Africa is like the golden sun that, having sunk beneath the western horizon, still plays upon the world which he sustained and enlightened in his career".

He then charged:

"Yes, the regeneration of Africa belongs to this new and powerful period!"

Dear Ayesha,

The point here is that black voices were not organized but they were all aspiring for self-determination, equal rights and respect for black people everywhere. So, when the Trinidadian barrister, Henry Sylvester Williams called a meeting in London in July 1900, his objective was to coordinate the sentiments that were brewing. The Anglo-Boer War in South Africa at the turn of the century had stirred up the expectations of peoples of African descent.

"I felt that it was time some effort was made to have us recognized as a people and so enable us to take our position in the world".
– Henry Sylvester Williams

Thirty-seven delegates, with 10 observers, from Africa, UK and the USA, was a good starting point. A while liberal Bishop Alexander Walters of the AME Zion Church was there to chair the meeting and to show solidarity at the Westminster Town Hall. African American scholar and civil rights activist, William Edward Burghardt Du Boi, was there to take notes. It was he who drafted the address to "The Nations of the World", directed to European leaders. The message: to grant colonies in Africa and the West Indies the right to self-government and political and other rights to African Americans. And equally important: to abolish racism.

The response of the British Colonial Secretary Joseph Chamberlain to the message was swift: *'Black people are totally unfit for representative institutions'*. It was shocking but not unexpected. The spirit of the blacks did not die.

Dear Ayesha,

So, you see, African Americans were not thinking only of themselves; they were also concerned about Africans being given the right to self-determination as far back as 1900. WEB Du Bois

142

did stop there; he went ahead to organize other conferences, and the next venue was Paris in 1909.

This time, 57 delegates from 15 countries, most of them residing in France, attended the conference. Significantly 21 came from the Caribbean, 16 from the United States, and 12 came from nine African countries. Why was it significant? The black world was gathering serious. They wanted colonialism and racism out of Africa and equality for all throughout the world.

The *"New York Evening Globe"* of February 12, 1919 said of the 1919 conference : *'the first assembly of the kind of history, and has for its object the drafting of an appeal to the Peace Conference to give the negro race of Africa a chance to develop unhindered by other races."*

It was this sense of brotherhood and collaboration among peoples of African descent that gained currency and came to be called **Pan-Africanism.**

Dear Ayesha,

More conferences and meetings went on in different venues, and on August 29, 1921, a London Manifesto was issued. Calling themselves Suppressed Races, the delegates called, among other demands, for *'civilized men'* to be recognized as *"civilized despite their race and color*; education in self-knowledge, in scientific truth and in industrial technique *'un-divorced from the art of beauty';* and *'the ancient common ownership of land and its natural fruits and defence against the unrestrained greed of invested capital'.*

Did you hear that? Delegates were asking 'civilized men' to give equal respect to other 'civilized people irrespective of their race and color.

As far back as 1921, delegates to these conferences were interested in uniting the whole of the African diaspora and gaining political rights for those on the continent. They were agitating for absolute equality of races.

Dear Ayesha,

I hope you now understand why Africans on the continent and those in the diaspora should understand each other, love each other and work together for common good. I believe that it is ignorance that has created the gap amongst both sides- those in the diaspora and those on the continent. It is in pursuit of this that when Ghana gained independence in 1957, President Kwame Nkrumah invited Dr Du Bois to Ghana to start compiling and publishing the *Encyclopeadia Africana.* It was a demonstration of the continuation of the construction of this common relationship. But more of this later.

My dear Ayesha,

It is true that at some point, Socialism and Marxist ideology was introduced into Pan-Africanism, but this should be seen in the context of the Cold War that enveloped the world and made choices appear to be either towards the Communist or Socialist East or the Capitalist West. This even later affected all liberation movements seeking to be self-reliant or non-aligned. But let's go back to Pan-Africanism. Ideologies mattered to give grounding and political character to the struggle being waged. It was not a secret that Socialist countries tended to support liberation groups in all parts of the world, especially in Africa.

Between the two World Wars, new names appeared on the scene. George Padmore, a journalist originally from Trinidad, migrated to the United States and studied there, and became a symbol and mentor for anti-imperialism and freedom in the Caribbean and Africa. At Ghana's independence in 1957, George Padmore was invited to Ghana as advisor to President Kwame Nkrumah until his death in 1959. A national library is named after him in Accra, Ghana.

Dear Ayesha,

The Congresses held in London and Lisbon in 1927 brought in 13 countries with 208 delegates. Twenty-two American states were represented, which was huge. African delegates came from the Gold Coast, Sierra Leone, Liberia and Nigeria. As eminent African-American scholar Molefi Kente Asante records, resolutions and demands favoring Africa included the following: *a voice in their own government; native rights to the land and its natural resources; modern education for all children; the development of Africa for the Africans and not merely for the profit of Europeans; and the reorganization of commerce and industry so as to make the main object of capital and labor the welfare of the many rather than the enriching of the few.*

Question is: were the colonial governments listening? The answer is yes, and that such demands were coming directly from the people in the colonies. The history of the various countries in the colonies, as well as the struggle for equal rights in America and the Caribbean show that there were agitations and nationalist uprisings in all countries where racism and colonialism persisted.

Dear Ayesha,

A lot of writing was going on at the same time despite the fact that black writers were facing difficulties having their scripts accepted by publishers most of whom were white and unsympathetic. Writers, intellectuals and activists who emerged included Jamaica-born Marcus Garvey, Isaac Theophilus Akunna Wallace-Johnson from Sierra Leone, Frantz Fanon from Martinique, Aime Cesaire from Martinique, Walter Rodney from Guyana, Cyril Lionel Robert James from Trinidad, and Cheikh Anta Diop from Senegal.

By the time for the 1945 Pan Africanist Congress organized in Manchester by WEB Du Bois, a new wave of black writers had joined forces with the crusade to see Africa united and the black race liberated from white supremacy. They included Langston Hughes and James Baldwin from America and Ladipo Solanke of Nigeria.

WEB Du Bois himself was immensely assisted by Mrs. Amy Jacques Garvey, wife of Marcus Garvey, a Jamaican doctor, Dr. Harold Moody. and other activists.

Political activists from the continent of Africa who were emerging included Kwame Nkrumah of Ghana, Ahmed Ben Bella of Algeria, Julius Nyerere of Tanzania, Patrice Lumumba of Congo, Amilcar Lopes da Costa Cabral of Guinea Bissau, Ahmed Sekou Toure of Guinea, and Peter Abraham of South Africa, Hastings Banda of Malawi and Obafemi Awolowo of Nigeria.

American singer and actor Paul Robeson, who was also influential, is quoted in Professor Sterling Stuckey's book, **Slave Culture,** as stating in 1934 : *"In my music, my plays, my films, I want to carry always this central idea-**to be African.** Multitudes of men have died for less worthy ideals; it is even more eminently worth living for.'*

Dear Ayesha,

The central message of Pan Africanism around the time revolved around the famous words of WEB Du Bois:

'When once the blacks of the US, the West Indies and Africa work and think together, the future of the black man in the modern world is safe'.

WEB Du Bois	*George Padmore*

It was the rallying platform for the African struggle for freedom and independence from colonial rule.

Dear Ayesha,

Trade Unions and Political organizations from Barbados, Bermuda, Saint Kitts, Jamaica, Grenada, Trinidad and Tobago, British Guiana, Liberia, Gambia, Nigeria, Cameroons, Sierra Leone, South Africa and the Gold Coast attended the Congress. Presided over by W. E. B. Dubois and Peter Milliard, the meeting had as joint secretaries Kwame Nkrumah of the Gold Coast, Jomo Kenyatta of Kenya and Peter Abrahams of South Africa.

This was a grouping of more than 200 delegates representing the United States of America, the Caribbean, and the continent of Africa. Liberia, Haiti and Ethiopia, whose flags were displayed at the venue were already independent.

What an assembly of black leaders determined to effect change in the lives and status of their people!

Dear Ayesha,

The topics for discussion and the eventual resolutions confirmed all expectations. The *Colour Problem* was one. The other was *Imperialism in North and West Africa.*

All the delegates identified with the equal civil, political, economic and social rights demands of over 13 million blacks in the United States of America, and urged for intensification of the struggle.

While the conference assured the governments of Ethiopia, Haiti and Liberia of solidarity and all support necessary, *immediate independence* was demanded for British and French West Africa, the British Sudan, the French North African colonies of Algeria, Tunisia and Morocco as well as Libya under Italian occupation.

My dear Ayesha,

I wish to emphasize that what I want you to take away from all these conferences is that they showed solidarity among a people who had faced together all the pains of slavery, colonialism, racism and loss of dignity as human beings.

For those from the United States and the Caribbean, Emancipation had been proclaimed but black people did not share the same rights as white people.

In Africa, aside of Liberia and Ethiopia, the rest of the countries were under European colonialism and imperialism.

Note also, that some key delegates to this 1945 Manchester Congress eventually went back to lead or assist in nationalist agitations for independence in their various countries.

In Nigeria, Chief Obafemi Awolowo subsequently became the prime minister of Western Nigeria; Dr Hastings Banda became the first prime minister of Nyasaland and later first President of the Republic of Malawi; and Peter Abrahams, a writer and activist from South Africa later settled in Jamaica and brought out to the world the cruel injustices of Apartheid in his books.

Chief Kenyan delegate, Jomo Kenyatta, left London to join in the struggle for independence from the British in his country, and became the first black prime minister and later first president of the Republic of Kenya.

Jomo Kenyatta of Kenya

"God said this is our land, land in which we flourish as people... we want our cattle to get fat on our land so that our children grow up in prosperity; and we do not want the fat removed to feed others..." **- Jomo Kenyatta .**

At the 1945 Manchester Pan-African Congress, Ghana's contingent included Joe Appiah and Dr Korankye Taylor, J.C. De Graft Johnson, Kankam Boadu, Eddie Duplan, and Ako Adjei who all played different roles in Ghanaian politics.

It was the joint secretary of the conference, Kwame Nkrumah, who eventually emerged as the founder of the Convention People's Party, which spearheaded the independence of Ghana. Nkrumah became the first prime minister of the Gold Coast, and later the first President of the Republic of Ghana.

In 1961, he was to write in his book, ***I Speak of Freedom***:

"Divided we are weak; united, Africa could become one of the greatest forces for good in the world. I believe strongly and sincerely that with the deep-rooted wisdom and dignity, the innate respect for human lives, the intense humanity which is our heritage, the African race, united under one federal government, will emerge not as just another world bloc to flaunt its wealth and strength, but as a Great Power whose greatness is indestructible because it is built not on fear, envy and suspicion, nor at the expense of others, but founded on hope, trust, friendship and directed to the good of all mankind."

Kwame Nkrumah

Dear Ayesha,
   Remember these statements:

   'No Black Man, let him be American, European, West Indian or African, shall be truly respected until the race as a whole has emancipated itself.' - Marcus Garvey

   'There are two things I had a right to - liberty or death. If I could not have one, I would have the other, for no man should take me alive. I should fight for my liberty as long as my strength lasted.' - Harriet Tubman

   I will be back, Ayesha.

   Efo Kojo

Chapter 11

FACING THE TRUTH

(Civil Rights in America)

"I refuse to accept the view that mankind is so tragically bound to the starless midnight of racism and war that the bright daybreak of peace and brotherhood can never become a reality…. I believe that unarmed truth and unconditional love will have the final word." —Martin Luther King, Jr.

My dear Ayesha,

It was the wife of the great Martin Luther King, Coretta Scott King who said:

"Hate is too great a burden to bear. It injures the hater more than it injures the hated."

An African proverb from Uganda also says:
"The one who loves you does not spare you the truth.

You must have heard of 'somebody' called Jim Crow.

No? I will tell you. There was this white actor, Thomas Rice, who before the abolition of slavery was performing a minstrel under a fictional name 'Jim Crow', a caricature of clumsy dimwitted black slave. So, it was a derogatory term for blacks until the late 19ᵗʰ century when it was used as a blanket term for anti-black laws. Note that these laws came after blacks had helped America to build itself into a nation – the period of Reconstruction as they call it.

Dear Ayesha,

Imagine that the same blacks who had endured severe inhuman treatment over one hundred years and had contributed to the economic reconstruction of America are the ones now being referred to in derogatory and nasty terms. Yes, this is exactly what happened.

Now, what were some of the laws that were passed and referred to as 'Jim Crow' laws?

Wait a minute, *Ayesha !*

Let me tell you about some laws passed in the Southern States before "Jim Crow". They called them the 'Black Codes'. Curfews were imposed on blacks across board. Blacks who were unemployed were to be jailed if they were found in town. If they wanted to live in the town they had to have white sponsors or passes from their employers. (*In Africa, you must know this was familiar in apartheid southern Africa!*)

Under the Black Codes, blacks could not hold any meetings, even church services. Forced labor or jail for those who violated these codes. Really?

So, what about the so-called Civil Rights Act of 1866 and the Fourteenth and Fifteenth Amendments we were taught in school in Africa? Under these Amendments, **black men** were to enjoy full citizenship, could vote, and were promised equal protection under the law. But 10 years later, after Federal troops had been withdrawn from the South, the repression continued.

Wait a minute, *Ayesha.*

There was also the Thirteenth Amendment. The 13th Amendment to the U.S. Constitution, ratified in 1865 in the aftermath of the Civil War, states: *"Neither slavery nor involuntary servitude,* ***except as a punishment for crime whereof the party shall have been duly convicted,*** *shall exist within the United States, or any place subject to their jurisdiction."*

My understanding of this clause is that as soon as you **are convicted as a criminal,** the conditions for *slavery* still hang on you. So you start asking yourself if you are an African from the continent : has slavery ended in America ?

Dear Ayesha,

Truth is that while these Amendments were being passed, the focus was on citizenship and the right to vote, not on the dignity of blacks as first class citizens. Not to affect racial segregation. The derisive Jim Crow laws in the late 1880s in the Southern States confirmed this.

The Legislative General Assembly of **Louisiana** had 16 members in 1890, and it passed a law to prevent black and white people from riding together on railroads. The Supreme Court upheld it and said that public facilities could be 'separate' but 'equal'.

In Mississippi and Louisiana, it soon became law to limit the voting right to only those 'who owned property or could read well".

In **South Carolina**, black and white textile workers could not work in the same room, enter through the same door, or gaze out of the same window. Many industries wouldn't hire blacks: Many unions passed rules to exclude them.

Dear Ayesha,
I know you are shocked and surprised. But read on.

In **Richmond, Virginia**, one could not live on a street unless most of the residents were people one could marry. Which means you could not marry someone from a different race.

In **Texas**, there were six entire towns where blacks could not live. There was curfew for blacks; they could not leave their homes after 10pm. 'Whites Only" or "Colored" were common signs on doors, ticket windows and drinking fountains.

Signs on the wall

Now, listen to this, *Ayesha*:

In most parts of the South, prisons, hospitals, and orphanages were segregated as were schools and colleges.

In **North Carolina**, black and white students had to use separate sets of textbooks.

In **Florida**, the books couldn't even be stored together. **Atlanta** courts kept two Bibles: one for black witnesses and one for whites.

"It shall be unlawful for a negro and white person to play together or in company with each other in any game of cards or dice, dominoes or checkers."—**Birmingham, Alabama, 1930"**

"Marriages are void when one party is a white person and the other is possessed of one-eighth or more negro, Japanese, or Chinese blood."—**Nebraska, 1911**

"Separate free schools shall be established for the education of children of African descent; and it shall be unlawful for any colored child to attend any white school, or any white child to attend a colored school."—**Missouri, 1929**

"All railroads carrying passengers in the state (other than street railroads) shall provide equal but separate accommodations for the white and colored races, by providing two or more passenger cars for each passenger train, or by dividing the cars by a partition, so as to secure separate accommodations."—**Tennessee, 1891**

Georgia had black and white parks. **Oklahoma** had black and white phone booths.

In **Virginia**, fraternal social groups with black and white members could not address each other as "Brother."

You wonder if any whites were carrying Bibles in these parts of America.

Dear Ayesha,

When fellow South Africans and Namibians are telling their story, just keep in mind what was happening in what was called the New World.

You must not be surprised if suicides, mental cases and violent behavior happened to a number of Africans, and their children, who could not bear these conditions.

So how did whites expect black people to behave? One commentator says a black person needn't do anything at all to be victimized; if a whitw person simply didn't like the look of a black person, that African American could lose everything, including his life.

Another commentator put it this way:

Black people who carried themselves with dignity, thrived economically, pursued education, dared to exercise their right to vote or rejected the sexual advances of whites could all be targets of white racism.

Dear Ayesha,

There is a limit to how far situations like these can be tolerated. What is known as the civil rights movement in America is the struggle that began publicly in the middle of the 20th century to seek social justice and equal rights. It included some white and other colored people who were now being segregated against.

A major story happened on December 1, 1955. A 42-year old African American woman named Rosa Parks found a seat on a Montgomery, Alabama bus after work. Because segregation laws stated that blacks must sit in designated seats at the back of the bus, Rosa complied accordingly.

Then, a white man came on the bus. He didn't find a seat in the white section at the front of the bus; so, the bus driver instructed Rosa Parks and three other blacks to give up their seats. Parks REFUSED and she was arrested.

Dear Ayesha,

The single act of Rosa Parks ignited the outrage and the spirit of defiance that gave the civil rights movement a character. Black community leaders, led by Baptist Minister Martin Luther

King, Jr., had formed the Montgomery Improvement Association (MIA); they immediately called for a boycott of the Montgomery bus system. This lasted 381 days, after which the Supreme Court in November 14, 1956 ruled that segregated seating was unconstitutional. One major victory won!

During this time, on the continent of Africa, the agitation for freedom, justice and national independence was very high. Riots and arson were regularly reported. In East and Central Africa, in Southern Africa, and in West Africa, British and French domination of the life of the people was being challenged and contested and quiet negotiations were on-going for eventual hand over to local leaders.

Dear Ayesha,

Agitations and protests for equal access to education and free movement of blacks and other colored people continued in other parts of the country until the **Civil Rights Act** was passed in 1957, the same year in which Ghana became the first country in black Africa to gain independence. The law allowed federal prosecution of anyone who tried to prevent someone from voting.

It empowered federal officials to prosecute individuals that conspired to deny or abridge another citizen's right to vote. Moreover, it also created a six-member U.S. Civil Rights Commission charged with investigating allegations of voter infringement. But, perhaps most importantly, the Civil Rights Act of 1957 signaled a growing federal commitment to the cause of civil rights. In Ghana, the jubilation was very high because, at least, the African had won his struggle to gain political independence from the British.

Certainly, the Civil Rights Act was not the end of protests, riots and demonstrations in America.

Thank you, President Dwight Eisenhower, but….!

Protests continue where there is injustice

My dear Ayesha,

On several fronts, blacks gathered, mobilized, organized and got their voices heard. Despite making some gains, blacks still experienced blatant prejudice in their daily lives. A Student Nonviolent Coordinating Committee was formed to drive all students into the struggle for civil rights.

Dear Ayesha,

Before I tell you about the great March on Washington in 1963, organized by known leaders such as A. Philip Randolph, Bayard Rustin and Martin Luther King, let me tell you about some women who haven't had much exposure.

Reading through the February 16, 2018 edition of USA Today, I came across names of women you should know who played key roles in the civil rights movement. Daisy Bates led the movement to end segregation in Arkansas in 1958. She was there at the March on Washington. Women fought relentlessly against racism and sexism. Ericka Huggins, a former leader of the Black Panther Party. Coretta Scott King was in her own right a great singer who sang to raise funds for her husband's movement. Ella Baker was active on the executives of the National Association for the Advancement of Colored People (NAACP) and the Student Nonviolent Coordinating Committee (SNCC).

Coretta Scott King

Ella Baker : Credit USA Today/AFP

Dear Ayesha,

On 28th August, 1963, more than 200,000 people, black and white, marched on Washington to send a message to President John F. Kennedy: for a comprehensive civil rights bill that would do away with segregated public accommodations; mechanism for seeking redress of violations of constitutional rights; protection of the right to vote, and desegregation of all public schools.

Signatories to these demands included the National Association for the Advancement of Colored People (NAACP), the National Urban League (NUL), National Council of the Churches of Christ in America, and the United Auto Workers (UAW). These, in addition to the Negro American Labor Council (NALC), the Southern Christian Leadership Conference (SCLC), the Congress of Racial Equality (CORE), and the Student Nonviolent Coordinating Committee (SNCC).

What this list means is that all these organizations which had been active in a number of initiatives in the past years considered

161

it was appropriate to commemorate the centennial of the Emancipation Proclamation of 1863. A lot of speeches were heard that evening, but evidently, the speech that made the headlines and has captured a place in history is the one made by Martin Luther King, Jr, *"I have a Dream"*.

Martin Luther King

Part of the speech says:

"Now is the time to make justice a reality for all of God's children. It would be fatal for the nation to overlook the urgency of the moment. ... The whirlwinds of revolt will continue to shake the foundations of our nation until the bright days of justice emerge.....

"I have a dream today ... I have a dream that one day every valley shall be exalted, every hill and mountain shall be made low... The rough places will be made plain, and the crooked places will be made straight.....And the glory of the Lord shall be revealed, and all flesh shall see it together. This is our hope....".

Dear Ayesha,

Reading through '*An Easy Burden*", a book presented to me by its author Andrew Young, himself a member of the Southern Christian Leadership Conference (SCLC), I appreciate where the inspiration of Martin Luther King's moving speech came from : *"Our religion taught us that we too were created in the image of God...and that we were endowed by our Creator with certain unalienable rights".* Andrew Young says further:
"We dared to believe that America could be healed of the gangrene of racism".

The Civil Rights Act of 1964 did not end the struggle for equal rights. Neither did revolts and riots stop. The emergence of Malcolm X and the Nation of Islam, the impact of Rev Jesse Jackson and the Rainbow Coalition, the formation of the Black Panther Party, the cruel assassination of Martin Luther King in 1968, and many other events took the civil rights movements even further.

Consider that around the same time, on April 20, 1964, Nelson Mandela was saying these words in jail in South Africa:

"During my lifetime I have dedicated myself to this struggle of the African people. I have fought against white domination, and I have fought against black domination. I have cherished the ideal of a democratic and free society in which all persons live together in harmony and with equal opportunities. It is an ideal which I hope to live for and to achieve. But if needs be, it is an ideal for which I am prepared to die".

Dear Ayesha,

The struggle was not yet over. There is a film you and your siblings and friends should look for and watch. It is entitled SELMA.

The film, which premiered on November 11, 2014, and is now popular around the world, tells the story of one other major event that led to the eventual passing of the Voting Rights Act of 1965.

Selma is a small city on the banks of Alabama River, with a population of some 22,000. It was city where less than one percent of potential black voters were registered. On Sunday, March 7, 1965, now referred to as "Bloody Sunday", some 600 African-Americans embarked on a march towards the state capital Montgomery to protest the shooting of a young black man, Jimmy Lee Jackson, by a state trooper and also to press home their demand for the right to vote. They were brutally attacked and assaulted by local police and white supremacists on the Edmund Petus Bridge with billy clubs and tear gas.

Dear Ayesha,

Two days later, civil rights activists led by Martin Luther King organized a 'symbolic' march towards the bridge, to raise awareness about black disenfranchisement. When they were met by local police, they knelt, prayed and sang the famous song, **We Shall Overcome**, after which they turned round back home. That night, three white pastors- James Reeb, Clark Olsen and Orloff Miller -who had come to join the solidarity march were brutally attacked by white supremacists using wooden clubs; Reverend Reeb died two days later.

Famous major-league baseball player, Jackie Robinson, decided to send a telegram to President Lyndon B. Johnson:
IMPORTANT YOU TAKE IMMEDIATE ACTION IN ALABAMA. ONE MORE DAY OF SAVAGE TREATMENT BY LEGALIZED HATCHET MEN COULD LEAD TO OPEN

WARFARE BY AROUSED NEGROES. AMERICA CANNOT AFFORD THIS IN 1965. JACKIE ROBINSON

Dr Martin Luther King and other leaders then decided to obtain official state protection to do a third march to Montgomery. They won a federal court order to now march lawfully.

On Sunday March 21, 1965, over 3,000 marchers, including children, started the 54mile (12 miles a day) walk, attracting 25,000 more participants, and reached Montgomery to present their petition. The leaders included Ralph Abernathy, Hosea Williams and Congressman John Lewis.

President Lyndon B. Johnson, with Dr King on hand, saw the opportunity to yield to black demands in June 1965. He signed the Voting Rights Act, saying it was *'...a triumph for freedom as huge as any victory that has ever been won on any battlefield'*.

Dr Martin Luther King made a statement 19 months before the signing of the Voters Rights Act:

"Now is the time to make real the promises of democracy.

Now is the time to rise from the dark and desolate valley of segregation to the sunlit path of racial justice.

Now is the time to lift our nation from the quicksands of racial injustice to the solid rock of brotherhood.

Now is the time to make justice a reality for all of God's children".

Dear Ayesha,

When I was your age in the 1960s, some of the popular pieces of music that came out of blacks in the diaspora were labeled *Negro Spirituals*. Incidentally, the term 'spiritual' is sometimes referred to as a derivation from 'spiritual song' from the King James Bible's translation of Ephesians 5:19, which says, '*Speaking to yourselves in psalms and hymns and spiritual songs, singing and making melody in your heart to the Lord".*

"Go Down Moses"
"Swing Low Sweet Chariot"
"Down by the Riverside"
"Sometimes I feel like a Motherless child".

These songs were originally sung during the first half of the 19th century when black slaves were building the underground railroads of America. It was illegal to teach slaves how to read and write, so they created coded messages in song. For example, '*Go Down Moses'* had these words:

"When Israel was in Egypt's land
Let my People go
Oppressed so hard they could not stand
Let my people go.
Refrain:
Go Down, Moses
Way down in Egypt's land
Tell Old Pharaoh
Let my people go".

For them as African slaves, they represented *Israel*, in the land of the slave master (*Pharaoh* or *Egypt*).

Whether they were sung by popular singers like Paul Robeson, Jessy Norman, Thomas Dorsey or Harvey Watkins, the messages, the melodious voices and the spirituality of the tone gave away the African in struggle. Freedom to be treated like everybody else in God's image has been a lasting battle cry.

167

My dear Ayesha,

Let me leave you with these words from Martin Luther King and Oprah Winfrey.

"I have a dream that my four little children will one day live in a nation where they will not be judged by the color of their skin but by the content of their character." — **Martin Luther King, Jr**

"I was raised to believe that excellence is the best deterrent to racism or sexism. And that's how I operate my life." — **Oprah Winfrey**

Be confident, Ayesha. Dream positive. Aim at Excellence!

You may also sing the song which we sang several times in our youth, **We Shall Overcome,** originally sung by tobacco workers:

We shall overcome, we shall overcome
We shall overcome someday
Oh, deep in my heart, I do believe
We shall overcome someday

The Lord will see us through, The Lord will see us through
The Lord will see us through someday
Oh, deep in my heart, I do believe
We shall overcome someday

We're on to victory, We're on to victory
We're on to victory someday
Oh, deep in my heart, I do believe
We're on to victory someday

We'll walk hand in hand, we'll walk hand in hand
We'll walk hand in hand someday
Oh, deep in my heart, I do believe
We'll walk hand in hand someday

We are not afraid, we are not afraid
We are not afraid today
Oh, deep in my heart, I do believe………
We are not afraid today
The truth shall set us free , the truth shall set us free
The truth shall set us free someday
Oh, deep in my heart, I do believe
The truth shall set us free someday

We shall live in peace, we shall live in peace
We shall live in peace someday
Oh, deep in my heart, I do believe
We shall live in peace someday

Efo Kojo

For My People

For my people everywhere,
Singing their slave songs
   repeatedly:
Their dirges and their ditties and their blues
   and jubilees,
Praying their prayers nightly to an
   unknown god,
Bending their knees humbly to an
   unseen power;
For my people lending their strength to the years, to the
   gone years and the now years and the maybe years,
Washing ironing cooking scrubbing sewing mending
   hoeing plowing digging planting pruning patching
Dragging along, never gaining, never reaping, never
   knowing and never understanding.

(*Poem by **Margaret Walker***)

Chapter 12

THE MINDS OF AFRICA

Knowing your history is empowering. And Africa stands poised on the birth of resurgence, a new renaissance. – **Professor Henry Louis Gates Jr., Harvard University**

My dear Ayesha,

At the age of 28, a Ghanaian philosopher named William E. Abraham published a book in 1962 entitled *"The Mind of Africa"*, and he is proud to say in the preface that Dr Kwame Nkrumah read the entire script before it was published. He emphasized in the book that it is the values of a society that constitute the material strength of its being.

Commenting on the book in the Foreword to the 2014 edition of the book, Professor Kwame Gyekye of the University of Ghana, clarified major the theme of *"The Mind of Africa"* by saying : *"If the new independent African nations are to evolve appropriate and credible ideologies to guide the development of their societies, they must take a serious and critical look at their own values, without necessarily discarding some of the values they must have acquired from decades of colonial contact".*

Dear Ayesha,

What these top African philosophers are saying is that we need to go back and study critically what our indigenous systems and way of life were, evaluate them and integrate what we find positive with whatever we have borrowed from elsewhere. In other words, we should not throw away our traditional way of doing things and blindly copy and own what Europeans have taught us in school.

As Africans, we have a pattern of behavior that is different from how other people of different cultures conduct themselves. They way we react to the environment, the way we communicate our expressions, the way we respect and honor our ancestors. It is the worth we give to what we believe in and imbibe as part of our way of life that we call Values. Our personal values, religious values, social values, our moral values, all these constitute aspects of our culture.

Dear Ayesha,

Our traditions, or what is sometimes referred to as our cultural heritage, include our institutions, our religion, the way we cope with the environment, and many more. As one of our learned Professor Kofi Abrefa Busia wrote: *"Every culture represents unique answers by a people to certain questions in the context of a particular historical situation".*

Dear Ayesha,

Our culture and values give us our identity. I want you to carefully listen to my older brother Kofi Asare Opoku, a professor in Africana Studies that I am never tired of reading:

"For many centuries, our ancestors lived here on this continent grounded in the knowledge and understanding of themselves as a people and of the world in which they lived. Without this knowledge, they could not have survived as a people who created their own unique societies, civilizations and cultures, established states, kingdoms and empires and came up with their own reflections and insights into the problems of the meaning life and death".

Of course, we have indigenous knowledge. Otherwise how would our ancestors have lived? It is this knowledge you and your peers will have to acquire. It is no secret that the tremendous progress made by countries in Asia and the Pacific is due mainly to the grounding they have in their own cultures and indigenous knowledge. They are using this knowledge to solve complex contemporary problems of development.

Moreover, it is of inestimable worth to those who plan and seek solutions to complex contemporary problems of development and progress in our country and our continent.

Dear Ayesha,

In March, 2018, the African University College of Communications (AUCC) organized an event to name the Africana Studies Center after the foremost African ethnomusicologists Professor Emeritus JH Kwabena Nketia who, at the age of 95 had gifted all his works to the university. The university invited as Guest Speaker one of the world's leading scholars in Africana Studies, Professor Molefi Kete Asante from Temple University in Pennsylvania. He chose as theme, *"This River is From Long Ago: Imagining a New African Studies Future"*.

Bearing a royal chief's title of Nana Okru Asante Peasah, Kyidomhene of Akyem Tafo, Molefi Kete Asante shook the 1,500seater National Theatre auditorium with a profound statement: **that the white images that have clouded Africa have contributed to the marginalization of the people from their own culture**.

Professor Asante pointed out a truth that most African people should know: that the Greeks are not the first philosophers, since Greece did not exist before Egypt, Nubia, India or China.

In his view, the tragedy today is that some of our youth in the African diaspora, especially our boys, have abandoned the arena of intellectual competition and allowed racist educational programs to divide Africans in their search for renaissance. Yes, the youth should join in the search for the truth and not leave the field to only Europeans.

Dear Ayesha,

As Molefi Asante emphasizes,

"We did not have to wait till the Greeks came to build the pyramids, the dzimbabwes, the Eredo fortification, or to master herbs, sciences, planting, organization, and numbers".

No doubt, emphasis on going back to re-learn our history, our arts and sciences, our herbs and our values keeps resonating.

Dear Ayesha,

Early 2017, I had listened to an interview granted a giant in African history, Professor Henry Louis Gates Jr. of Harvard University on Public Broadcasting Service (PBS) in the United States of America. It was Black History Month, and PBS used the opportunity to discuss Professor Gates's six-part documentary series entitled, *"Africa's Great Civilizations".*

My dear Ayesha,

Tell your lecturers that I wish all universities and high schools on the continent of Africa and in the diaspora would make these series available in the classrooms and lecture theatres.

It took Professor Gates five years, traveling through 12 African countries, to produce a six-hour program that covers 200,000 years of African history.

Admitting that images of Africa in his childhood came from Tarzan and Ramar and Sheema of the jungle, and that embarrassed him greatly, he made a conscious effort to know more about the continent after he was 19. The series he has created tells the story about Africa, home of the world's most ancient civilizations.

Dear Ayesha,

Most of what I have already told you is now captured on film. Professor Gates confirms that the achievements of Africa have been **obscured** – *"first of all because of history; and then after 1884 was the Berlin Conference when European powers sat* *down, looked at an empty map of Africa, and basically carved it up like you carve up a pizza pie".*

Dear Ayesha,

I would like you to listen once again to this truth about Africa told by Louis Gates:

"So, they had to create a fiction of Africa as an empty place or a static place full of primitive people who were stuck in time. And those were ostensibly our ancestors.

"But the pre-colonial world knew all about Africa. There wasn't a moment really since the ancient Egyptians when Northern Africa, the Mediterranean world and the larger world wasn't in touch with African civilizations, with some part of Africa."

Ayesha, tell this to your tutor*:*

"The Red Sea was a highway. The Nile was a highway. The Sahara was a highway, particularly after the domestication of camels, and the Indian Ocean highways.

"The emperor of great Zimbabwe ate off porcelain plates that came from China. That's the 13th century. It's incredible. Most of Europe's gold between 1000 A.D. and 1500 A.D. came from West Africa. All our history was stolen from us".

Why did they rob us of our history?

Professor Gates summarizes it all: *"We were robbed of a history because Europeans wanted to justify an economic order which depended upon our ancestors' exploitation".*

Dear Ayesha,

I know what is running through your mind: why are our history teachers not teaching us all this? Is it because they have not researched like the others? Or is it because they might lose their degrees because they used a different narration to obtain their certificates?

I believe there is no harm in re-learning, Ayesha.

175

It demands humility and a sense of purpose. The time of the mythic claims should be over. There are now hard facts about the history of Africa that every educated person across the continents should know about.

Dear Ayesha,

Remember this from Henry Louis Gates*:*

"Knowing your history is empowering. And Africa stands poised on the birth of resurgence, a new renaissance.

"And knowing about this rich and splendid history will be crucial to the individual self-esteem of every African and to the collective, as it were, sense of itself of the African people".

I love you, Ayesha.

Efo Kojo

Chapter 13

AFRICA HEALS ITSELF

"For tomorrow belongs to the people who prepare for it today"
– African Proverb

My dear Ayesha,
    There is no doubt that the African family has gone through pain and humiliation. But it is also true that the resilience of our people has held sway over the treatment given us. We have had leaders who have used violence in equal measure to regain their pride. We have examples in the Caribbean, in Africa and in North America. We also have had leaders who have chosen the non-violent path. Martin Luther King and Nelson Mandela come to mind. The question that I hear some of your peers asking is: apart from the color, what else binds the African people together? Or else, what do we have to bind us together? I have chosen a few areas to share with you, to help you educate yourself adequately. Malcolm X added on to the African proverb by saying: *"Education is the passport to the future, for tomorrow belongs to the people who prepare for it today"*.

Dear Ayesha,
    Our elders say: *"He who learns, teaches"*. All the history you are learning is expected to equip you, like all peoples of

African descent, to understand that you came from the same stock, thousands of years ago. This is one binding balm that should heal the pain we have suffered, and even continue to suffer in many instances. It is **our history** that gives us a self-esteem, a self-worth, to assure us that we can rise again. Call it regeneration, call it renaissance, call it rebirth. Africa shall rise again. **History unites us**.

Yes, Africa shall overcome

Dear Ayesha,

    Our culture heals and unites us. No matter the distance in time and space, meet an African and you do not need any introduction: his black skin - light to dark tone; broad nose, black wooly hair.

Respect for elders. Love of family. Africans love the communal spirit. We love meeting as family. We love hanging around our elders, our older people. Family reunions happen everywhere African people meet. That is why we love festivals; they are points of reuniting with ourselves and our ancestors. Non-Africans know that Africans love singing and dancing. Yes, it's because we express ourselves freely, much more easily than other people. It is an African thing.

When Africans meet as family, they also use the occasion to resolve conflicts. Elders use peaceful mechanisms to bring disputes to an end. No doubt there have been cultural shifts on both the continent and in the diaspora, but family integrity has been sustained. Through it, family values have been transmitted to the younger generation, despite challenges that the youth face with a pounding stream of other cultures.

Dear Ayesha,

Religion is next. No matter which religion one belongs to in Africa, we always find a common ground to live with and accommodate each other. Most religious riots are politically motivated. It was Alik Shahadah, Arabic film maker and scholar, who once said: *"Religion is a bottle with a label; spirituality is the thing inside. Religion is simply the culture of spiritual belief".* Before Africans were transported illegally across the Atlantic to the Americas or the Caribbean, they were familiar with African traditional religion, and a few of them had been christened or baptized in one or the other Christian church. What was most common on the seas and on land when they arrived was that they received teachings according to the Bible. Yet this situation did not take away the spirituality from them as Africans.

The African concept of God is understood in the existence of a Supreme Being living side by side with other spirit beings, the living-dead or ancestors. The spirits that possess African traditional priests are misunderstood and are wrongly called "fetish". We call our traditional priests by their name. We don't call them 'fetish priests'; they are traditional priests.

179

Dear Ayesha,

When Africans were dragged and put on ships to another world, they did not leave their faith in God behind. It is a combination of the rituals in the expression of their faith in the Supreme Being that has come to be called Voodoo. The name has been derived from the Afro-Caribbean word 'vodun' which means 'spirit'. Voodoo is therefore a mixture of practices from ethnic groups from Dahomey, Nigeria, Congo, Senegal, Angola, Libya, Malagasy, Ethiopia, and Sierra Leone, even with aspects of Christianity.

When Europeans don't understand it, they call it 'primitive', or 'fetish' and you hear some African scholars mimicking the same thinking. Voodoo is not fetish.

Dear Ayesha,

What should be of interest is why voodoo is not as widespread in America as in the Caribbean. In America, the English colonizers and settlers introduced their Anglican religion, which enslaved Africans associated with chattel slavery, bondage and servitude. Africans, as religious as they were, found that even their dancing was considered 'primitive'. They therefore found the new revival churches in America as more acceptable. They embraced the supremacy of a higher being and the teaching that men are equal in the sight of God; and even more in the message that 'all have sinned and fallen short of the glory of God". Africans saw more faith in the 'new hope' and 'rebirth' and 'liberation' that the revival churches preached. Hence the birth of the 'Negro Church' and association with revival churches in America.

Even in modern day America, as on the continent of Africa, more 'spiritual churches' are springing up and allowing free expression of praises in singing and dancing. It is an African thing. It is a **healing** mechanism.

Dear Ayesha,

Traditional medicine is healing lots of Africans. There is a certain movement of people asking for organic food these days.

Organic food is free from chemical fertilizers, pesticides, chemical additives and genetically modified organisms (GMOs). Research has shown that they provide more vitamins and antioxidants. These are foods that our ancestors ate long before the introduction of chemicals in our foods.

However, why I bring this up is that, even though Western medicine has come to save lives, our people have relied on organic plants, herbs and roots for thousands of years. You remember the medicinal and scientific feats of the ancient African civilization – they did not die. Our ancestors carried on with their scientific way of healing with our herbs and traditional medicine before the white man came.

My dear Ayesha,

I like a statement by Professor Kofi Asare Opoku of the African University College of Communications in Ghana: *"If our ancestors did not have medicines to combat the diseases that afflicted them, nor did they not have good food to eat to sustain them, then there would have been no reason for people to have been living in this part of the world; and those who claimed to have "discovered" us would have come to find only trees and animals here"*. Indeed, it supports the African proverb that says: *"Before the blacksmith forged his razor, the vulture and the guinea fowl shaved their heads"*.

Dear Ayesha,

The World Health Organization (WHO) estimates that about 80% of the population in developing countries in the world depend on traditional medicine, or what they call alternative medicine. Studies are revealing daily that African and Caribbean forests and home backyards have trees, plants and herbs which have immense medicinal value. Breakthroughs are reported daily from various parts of Africa and the Caribbean in the use and efficacy of traditional herbal and plant medicine. Of course, for various reasons, some Western countries do not recognize these herbs, but what is known is that the certified versions of the same herbs have found their way into the shops and homes of the people living there. There is the case of the discovery of a herbal drug called 'URO-500' for t the management of Benign Prostatic Hyperplasia (BPH), a non-malignant enlargement of the prostate gland by researchers from the Center for Scientific Research Into Plant Medicine in Ghana. Overnight, the Center has experienced a traffic jam never seen before, coming not only from Africa but from the rest of the world.

From Nigeria, consultant surgeon and lecturer, Dr. Spencer Efem, at the University Teaching Hospital in Calabar, Nigeria is reported to have successfully used honey straight from the beehive to treat wounds, including burns, deep bedsores and various types of ulcers. And the *New Scientist,* July 7, 1988, reports that, *"This is the first time that it has been demonstrated that honey can be used to remove dead tissues from persistent wounds instead of stripping it away surgically".*

In South Africa, the Cape Floral Kingdom in the Cape Province boasts of holding 4% of the world's plant species, equivalent of about 9000 plant species catering for research and manufacture of various plant and herbal products. Compare this to about 1,500 species in the whole of the United Kingdom. Because of its unparalleled biodiversity, with 70% of its plants being endemic only in the area, the Cape Floristic Region is declared a World Heritage Site.

Researches and production of herbal drugs continue in other parts of the continent, also in East and Central Africa, with 17 countries signed up for the African Medicinal Plants Standards (AMPS) based in Mauritius.

Dear Ayesha,

Did you hear President Paul Kagame of Rwanda taking about African solutions? *"Africa's story has been written by others; we need to own our problems and solutions and write our story."*.

Dear Ayesha,

It is widely known in the Caribbean that good herbal knowledge was obtained from Africans who were transported across the oceans during the slave trade. Just like in Africa, this knowledge was passed on by word of mouth until written information became available. In the Bahamas, for example, people on many of the islands depend on herbal or plant medicine. According to Martha Hanna-Smith, in her book '*Bush Medicine in Bahamian Folk Tradition'',* mental and physical illness is cured through bush medicine, as they call it. "*Bush medicine is given to infants as well as adults for both preventive as well as curative pur*poses".

Use of African Traditional Medicine among African communities worldwide is common knowledge. Indeed, **Africa heals** itself.

Dear Ayesha,

I dare say that **African achievements** in science, technology, sports, entertainment and academics constitute a huge healing medicine for peoples of African descent everywhere. It is a fact that, as usual, records and reports of black achievements have either been hidden or destroyed. Yet with time, most of these are emerging. The question is: why hide, displace or destroy somebody else's record of achievement? Ayesha, I hope you know the reason by now. It was the same way the truth about ancient African civilization was hidden for centuries.

Certain truths: Africans in most parts of the continent, in the various kingdoms and empires of the Pharaohs, Kongo, Shona, Ghana, Songhai, had knowledge and better use of metals, especially iron, before any contact with Europeans. Secondly, most of the Africans who were enslaved and brought into what was called the New World had not been through formal education. Thirdly, laws were put in place by authorities in the Southern states of America and most parts of the Caribbean not to allow Africans to be educated.

Dear Ayesha,

What this tells you is that blacks who became pioneer achievers in their various fields were really the true innovators, discoverers and inventors. It took quite a long time for Africans to get the recognition they deserved because of the environment in which they found themselves. In the early 1950's when Kwame Nkrumah launched the accelerated educational plan in Ghana, blacks in America were battling segregation laws. Today, the impression is given to African students who come from the continent to the United States that African Americans are 'lazy'. Yes, you will be told this to make you hate each other as blacks in America and think you are differently placed. It is part of the scheme to divide us.

Remember this African proverb, Ayesha: *"When brothers fight to their death, a stranger inherits their father's estate"*. You get the message?

Dear Ayesha,

Thomas Jennings was the first African American person to receive a patent in the U.S. in 1821 despite protestations from whites because of his color.

George Carruthers, an astrophysicist created the ultraviolet camera which NASA used when it launched Apollo 16 in 1972.

Dr Patricia Bath, an ophthalmologist, invented the device that refined laser cataract surgery, called Laserphaco Probe – the first female African American doctor to receive a medical patent, in 1988.

Find time to read Louis Haber's *"Black Pioneers of Science and Invention"*, and many other books, which list African achievers of the past. You will learn for example, that Garrett Morgan invented the gas mask and traffic lights; that Daniel Hale Williams performed the first open-heart surgery; and that Lewis Latimer was a pioneer in electrical lighting. Just imagine the contribution only these three pioneers made towards industrialization in the period of reconstruction in the United States. There are other hundreds of them.

My dear Ayesha,

Many more inventors have come out of the continent of Africa, and today several youths are giving us hope that our sense of innovation and creativity is making a difference in world development.

Sometimes I wonder where the world's biggest sport, the World Cup (Soccer) competition would be if there were no South American and African teams. Even in European teams, the glamour is provided by black players of African descent. Talk Basketball, Football, Baseball, Soccer, Golf and Boxing in America and Europe, and the top achievers make you proud. Certainly, these **achievements** heal Africa.

Dear Ayesha,

On June 13, 2019, history was unveiled in front of NASA Headquarters in Washington, DC. Three black Americans were honored after several decades for the major contribution they made to space travel in the United States and the world. Katherine Johnson, Dorothy Vaughan, and Mary Jackson, named 'the human computers', were the brains and mathematicians whose complex calculations made space travel possible in the late 50s into the 60s. The street in front of NASA Headquarters is named after the 'Hidden Figures'. So, why were the names hidden all these years ?

The truth could not be hidden any more !

Dear Ayesha,

Africa's rich mineral resources, not to talk of the huge talents we produce in sports, entertainment, science and technology, give us a lot of hope.

The National Geographic Society describes Africa as the "Mother Continent" being the oldest inhabited continent on earth. Humans and human ancestors have lived in Africa for more than 5 million years.

It was our mineral resources that led European countries to convene the 1844 meeting in Berlin to divide up Africa. It was over these resources that David Livingstone recommended the 3Cs – Commerce, Christianity and Civilization. Yes, so much exploitation of these resources has taken place, sometimes with connivance of certain African leaders. Without a doubt, Africa did not have capital to exploit these resources. In most cases, in newly independent African countries where the people were denied education, qualified human resource capability was limited.

Dear Ayesha,

The fact remains that the resources, and the market, that Africa possesses are the reasons why the major power blocks are virtually competing for political, economic, military and cultural positions on the continent. Let's feel proud that we have a continent that can feed the world.

Finally, Ayesha,

Now, we have a common history with all blacks wherever they find themselves. We have cultural similarities that we should explore and be proud of. Our spirituality in religion is common and we should not allow denominations to split us. We have medicinal plants, herbs and roots which heal the world. We share common philosophies of life handed to us by our ancestors; and above it all, we are owners and beneficiaries of a huge continent with a variety of natural, human and material resources. We have a reason to feel blessed.

What we now have to struggle for is a United States of Africa. Note this, Ayesha:

"The [Black] world therefore must be seen as existing not simply for itself but as a group whose insistent cry may yet become the warning which awakens the world to its truer self and its wider destiny". – WEB Du Bois

WEB Du Bois

And the African proverb: ***A family tie is like a tree, it can bend but it cannot break.***

And, also remember what the icon Oprah Winfrey said:

"Turn your wounds into wisdom."— Oprah Winfrey

Enjoy reading, Ayesha.

Efo Kojo

Chapter 14

RETURN TO JAMESTOWN, GHANA

"At long last, the battle has ended, and Ghana my beloved country is free forever"- Kwame Nkrumah

My dear Ayesha,

The last time we left the Pan African Conference in Manchester, in 1945, some of the delegates, particularly from Africa, had been fired up by the momentum that was gained.

Joint Secretary Jomo Kenyatta, who had been in the United Kingdom since 1931 and had met black activists like Kwame Nkrumah, Paul Robeson, Peter Abrahams and CLR James, eventually left for his home country, Kenya, in September 1946. He immediately assumed leadership of the Kenya African Union, which had been formed to oppose British control of Kenya.

Dear Ayesha,

Note that Kenya was part of the portions of Africa that was handed over to the British after the 1884 Berlin conference. Economic disparities between the British settlers and the Africans led to various forms of agitation by Kenyans.

A militant group within the Kikuyu ethnic group, the Mau Mau, emerged early 1950s and rebelled to remove European presence from Kenya. It stood violently against lack of access to land and low wages, among other injustices. Assassinations, murders, cases of arson and violence led to the British clamping down on leading nationalist leaders. Jomo Kenyatta, suspected to be an active member of the Mau Mau organization, was arrested in November, 1952, and flown to a prison in a remote district of Kapenguria. Open rebellions, closure of schools and violent arrests and wild killings of both British and Kenyans followed this action until Kenya became ungovernable. Thousands of Kikuyu tribesmen were either murdered or arrested and imprisoned by British troops.

When the British eventually wanted peace and called for a Constitutional Conference in London, the Nationalist leaders boycotted it, until Jomo Kenyatta was released a year later, on January 18, 1961.

The following year, 1962, Kenyatta led a Kenya National Union (KANU) team to London to negotiate for a Constitution that would lead Kenya into independence on December 12, 1963.

Dear Ayesha,

If you will remember, at the 1945 Manchester Pan-African Congress, Ghana's contingent included Kwame Nkrumah, Joe Appiah, Ako Adjei, Dr Korankye Taylor, J.C. De Graft Johnson, Kankam Boadu, and Eddie Duplan.

Prior to the Manchester meeting, Nkrumah had completed his Masters degree course in Divinity in the United States of America, from where he had associated himself with leading Pan-Africanists like WEB Du Bois and the agitation for Race Equality in America, and had formed the African Students Organization. He was in London to study Economics and Law.

However, in the United Kingdom, black students mainly from the British colonies had also formed themselves into the West African Students Union (WASU) as far back as 1925. Earlier members, mostly law students, included J.B. Danquah as first president, Solanke Ladipo as first secretary-general and J.E. Casely Hayford as the first patron. Their original objective was to seek the welfare of West African students who had migrated to the United Kingdom. Over time, WASU became the platform for discussing issues related to self-government and independence for African countries through the early 40s until Kwame Nkrumah arrived from America. Nkrumah probably found the WASU too conservative, and he formed a subgroup called the Circle, within it, to become the radical revolutionary vanguard. Using his connections with the Pan-African Federation and the World Federation of Trade Unions, he got involved with the organization of the 1945 fifth Pan-African Congress.

Dear Ayesha,

I hope you are following closely how Africans were also organizing themselves to free their countries from colonial domination. Kwame Nkrumah's dynamism won him the position of secretary-general of the West African National Secretariat which had been formed at the Manchester conference to coordinate the independence of West African states. He was soon to be elected vice -president of WASU, a further position that propelled his political career.

Meanwhile, the agitation for local representation in the legislative assembly in the Gold Coast had been going on from the 1920s. Law students who had studied in the United Kingdom and educated chiefs had all joined in the demand for inclusion in the making of laws. A mass political grouping emerged in 1947 called the United Gold Coast Convention (UGCC) with leading members as Joseph Boakye Danquah, Ernest Ako Adjei, Edward Akufo-Addo, William Ofori-Atta, and Emmanuel Obetsebi-Lamptey. The chairman was a wealthy merchant called George Paa Grant. Their slogan was "Self-Government within the shortest possible time".

Dear Ayesha,

It got to a point when the group agreed to a proposal that in order to inject some more energy into the organization, and to have a full-time administrator to move the group forward, Dr Kwame

Nkrumah was to be invited to head the secretariat. The proposal came from Kwame Nkrumah's colleague from the Manchester conference, Ernest Ako-Adjei.

Dear Ayesha,

I wish to stress the state of preparedness of Kwame Nkrumah to undertake this assignment. He was well equipped with the history of Africa. He was knowledgeable about Ancient African civilization and the old kingdoms of Ghana, Mali and Songhai. He had studied in America and about America. He had been a student activist. He had been a leader. He had studied world politics; he understood the dynamics of where the world was going. He was an organizer, a communicator and a strategic thinker. His colleagues in America and the United Kingdom could attest to his capabilities to lead. He was a grassroots person; despite his high education, he was modest and down-to-earth. He was a match in intellectual debates and a forceful and compassionate speaker. He was an internationalist of rare standing among his peers.

I believe that Kwame Nkrumah was himself waiting for this opportunity coming from Accra. He jumped at the offer and came home late 1947 from London to take over the UGCC as Secretary-General. Without a doubt, the tempo of the UGCC organization appeared slow for his liking; it had to change, and rather quickly. Mobilization of workers to protest against British rule was to continue. After only two months, the leaders of UGCC were arrested and imprisoned briefly in various locations throughout the country; they were held responsible for the looting and rioting that took place after the killing of some ex-servicemen marching through the streets of Accra in protest against their conditions.

Dear Ayesha,

When the leaders were released, following public protests, Kwame Nkrumah considered the formation of a Youth Group to accelerate the process towards independence. He formed the Committee on Youth Organization (CYO) and organized more strikes and boycotts throughout the country, winning more students, workers and farmers to the party. He also established a newspaper to become the organ of the independence movement.

It became evident that some leaders of the UGCC were not in favor of Kwame Nkrumah's strategies, and sharp disagreements were showing. The way out was for Kwame Nkrumah to break away from the UGCC which he considered elitist and conservative and form the Convention People's Party (CPP) as the grassroots organization.

My dear Ayesha,

Before I continue with what happened after the CPP was formed, let me take you to Jamestown in the early 50s as told by architect and historian Amarteifio at the Jamestown Café:

Nat Nuno-Amarteifio, Jamestown historian

Jamestown Cafe

Jamestown port

"The first decades of the 20th century saw the introduction of racially segregated neighborhoods in Accra. The establishment of the Gold Coast colony and the choice of Accra as its capital brought more Europeans to the town. Improvements in medicine made it possible for many of them to survive the diseases of the tropics. Several moved into stone houses in Jamestown. Colonialism and European imperialism that flourished at the end of the 19th century however invented toxic and repressive racial attitudes. The colonial administration made laws to remove the Europeans from the Ga communities and justified the decision on the grounds of reducing their appalling mortality rate. They built communities at the Ridge then Cantonment for the use of whites.

When British journalist Henry Stanley and explorer Mary Kingsley visited Accra at the end of the 19th century they both stayed at the Sea View Hotel. They wrote about Accra's changing urban landscape and mixture of mud huts and stone houses".

According to Nuno-Amarteifio:

"The Wesleyan Missionary Society established a boy's school in Jamestown in the 1840's. It was located at Sempe and still exists as a junior secondary school.

"The Wesleyan Boys School was the only school in Jamestown until 1886 when a government subsidized school was built there. In 1915 the first privately funded school, the Accra Royal School was opened in Jamestown.

The Methodist Cathedral is still a popular place of worship, among many other religious denominations in Jamestown. It has a word of inspiration on its walls:

'Your talent determines what you can do. Your motivation determines how much you are willing to do it. But your ATTITUDE determines how well you do it"

METHODIST CATHEDRAL, (1910) JAMESTOWN, ACCRA

"Jamestown's long and episodic history has left many monuments and architectural masterpieces. These can contribute handsomely to a tourist industry. The old Sea View Hotel is one the latest pieces of Jamestown still hanging. It is not in use as it used to be, and the historian Nuno Amarteifio hopes the new vibrant Jamestown Association will soon turn it into a major tourist attraction.

Jamestown. *Credit Allotey Bruce Konuah*

SEA VIEW HOTEL (FIRST HOTEL IN ACCRA, BUILT IN 1870), JAMESTOWN, ACCRA

As Allotey Bruce Konuah of Jamestown Café argues, *"Jamestown has a unique character – on land, and on the seashore*

– with people of different backgrounds". The community has been home to a number of politicians, academics, and lawyers; and before Kwame Nkrumah returned home in 1947, it was a vibrant center for social and political activities. All political parties were, and are still, well represented in Jamestown. Night life is a mixture of local pubs and street parties. Kwame Nkrumah was not a native of Jamestown but won elections in that constituency.

Dear Ayesha,

The British colonial authorities must have been quite amused to see a split among the same Gold Coasters asking for Self-Government. What was the difference? While UGCC was advocating for "Self-government within the shortest possible time, Kwame Nkrumah's CPP was shouting "Self-government Now!". There is no doubt that the British authorities had called for the full files and all the dossiers on Kwame Nkrumah's activities in the United States and in the United Kingdom. Here was the communist and socialist who had joined several workers and student organizations, spoken at various functions not just on independence for African countries but also in favor of racial equality for all blacks. Here was the friend of Marxists and leftist movements, rallying the youth, workers and farmers to pour into the streets to shake the foundations of colonial domination.

Kwame Nkrumah termed the non-violent agitations "Positive Action". The authorities would not have it. They felt the pressure mounting for the granting of independence to a determined people.

Kwame Nkrumah was arrested, charged with sedition, and sent to prison. His new location: **James Fort Prison**, Jamestown, Accra

James Fort Prison, Jamestown

Dear Ayesha,

Kwame Nkrumah was in jail in Jamestown when he won a seat in parliament to represent Accra Central; his party won the elections with a landslide, two-thirds majority in the Legislative Assembly. When he was eventually released, he became the first prime minister of the country, and led the nation to independence in 1957. Ghana became the first black African country to win the political battle against foreign domination.

This victory had become possible due to earlier struggles waged by ex-servicemen, farmers, chiefs, political activists, and many others who came before Nkrumah, as well as the political organizational skills which Kwame Nkrumah definitely had as a leader.

Equally significant was the internationalist solidarity Kwame Nkrumah enjoyed from many Pan-Africanists, civil rights leaders and trade unionists that he had worked with in Europe and the Americas.

Nkrumah released from James Fort Prison, Jamestown

On the day of the declaration of independence, Kwame Nkrumah told a large crowd in Accra:

"At long last, the battle has ended; And thus Ghana, your beloved country is free forever...

"As I said in the assembly just minutes ago, I made a point that we are going to create our own African personality and identity.

"It's the only way that we can show the world that we are ready for own own battles.

"But today, may I call upon you all – that on this great day, let us all remember that nothing in the world can be done unless it's had the purport and support of God.

"We have won the battle and we again re-dedicate ourselves ... Our independence is meaningless unless it is linked up with the total liberation of Africa.

"Let us now fellow Ghanaians, let us now ask for God's blessing and for only two seconds in your thousands and millions, I want to ask you to pause only for one minute and give thanks to almighty God for having led us through our difficulties,

imprisonments, hardships and suffering to have brought us to the end of our trouble today."

Dear Ayesha,

Prominent black leaders were invited by Kwame Nkrumah on March 6, 1957, to celebrate the independence with Ghana. Among these were Martin Luther and Coretta King. When he returned to the United States of America, Martin Luther King delivered a sermon on April 24th at Dexter Avenue Baptist Church, after which he read a personal message from Kwame Nkrumah:

"Our sympathies are with America and its allies. But we will make it clear through the United Nations and other diplomatic channels that beautiful words and extensive handouts cannot be substitutes for the simple responsibility of treating our colored brothers and sisters as first class human beings."

To which Martin Luther King added:

"So, if we are a first-class nation, we cannot have second-class citizens".

Dear Ayesha,

Kwame Nkrumah's vision was far beyond Ghana. It was demonstrated throughout his political life that the struggle for racial equality, justice, freedom and the unity of all blacks under a United States of Africa was the ultimate goal.

My dear Ayesha,

It was the Asantehene, King of the Asante kingdom, Nana Sir Osei Agyeman Prempeh II, who gave the distinguishing title, Ɔsagyefo, victorious leader, the incomparable one who saves in battle, to Kwame Nkrumah, when he became President of the Republic of Ghana, saying that Nkrumah *"had done so much for Ghana and Africa that he deserved this title"*.

Kwame Nkrumah became, from then, the icon of African Liberation.

Kwame Nkrumah left some indelible words for posterity:

'As far as I am concerned, I am in the knowledge that death can never extinguish the torch which I have lit in Ghana and Africa. Long after I am dead and gone, the light will continue to burn and be borne aloft, giving light and guidance to all people'.

With all my love.

Efo Kojo

Nelson Mandela: "It always seems impossible until it's done"

Chapter 15 (Epilogue)

❦

THE GIANT SHALL ARISE

"If you want to go quickly, go alone. If you want to go far, go together." - African Proverb

"No matter how long the night is, the morning is sure to come. (African proverb)"

My dear Ayesha,

I have found on our thus far that some historians would love to dispute the fact that the name Africa is *African*. They go around in circles ascribing the origin of the name to Greek and Roman writers. The truth is now known that Africa is an original Egyptian word "Afru-ika" meaning "Motherland". Africa is our motherland, the land where man, civilization and religion originated from.

Despite all the attempts made by the Greeks, Romans, and Europeans to erase the truth about the continent, Africa still rises, and will rise even higher. Our people fought in various battles and wars, survived the worst form of human treatment through slavery, the slave trade, and colonialism, but Africa stood defiant. Once the youth like you, Ayesha, are now fed with the true history, the absolute unification process of all peoples of African descent will begin to take shape.

You will find many arguments that unification is not possible because of multiplicity of languages and different political ideologies and systems. Tell those who argue that way that the United States of America, China, and Europe once had the same challenges. Sometimes, some of our own leaders, scholars and intellectuals argue the same way, but I ascribe it to lack of the knowledge of Africa's history. Or simply lack of confidence!

The symbol of the African Union

Dear Ayesha,

I believe we have come a long way to now understand that Africans who were divided by history and circumstances can be reunited. It is not a romantic dream hoping that African Americans or blacks in South America, Asia or in the Caribbean will move and come and live in Africa. Just as Euro-Americans feel proud and a belonging to Europe, so will blacks in America or Europe equally hold their chests high if the rich African continent is politically and economically united.

Dear Ayesha,

You must also be aware that people of African descent continue to struggle for racial equality and recognition as first-class citizens. 'Black Lives Matter' is a real phenomenon. Mass incarceration of people of color continues. Over two million people of color are in prison. There is a rising poverty rate and unemployment is still very high. These conditions cannot be separated from what is happening in some parts of the continent. For me, the ultimate solution is a strong United States of Africa.

Dear Ayesha,

Africa produces huge volumes of gold and diamonds. Botswana, Angola, South Africa, the Democratic Republic of the Congo, Liberia, Sierra Leone and Namibia are Africa's largest producers of diamonds. Africa also possesses large quantities of important metals and minerals such as uranium, used to produce nuclear energy; platinum, used in jewelry and industrial applications; nickel, used in stainless steel, magnets, coins, and rechargeable batteries; bauxite, a main aluminum ore; and cobalt, used in color pigments. Then there are vast forest and agricultural lands that can turn around the fortunes of the continent and make it a powerful force to reckon with.

Dear Ayesha,

On one of his visits to Ghana for an OAU meeting, Colonel Muamar Al Gaddafi of Libya told journalists:

"How can an African country face a Europe that is united, negotiate with the USA, Japan, or China…With a single government, Africa would be on an equal footing with them." He *said further, If the African masses are enlightened and aware, then Africa will come into being…those at the summit should hear the voice of the masses."*

Colonel Gaddafi made a very important point that if Africa developed its resources under one government, Africa would create jobs for its jobless youth and reduce the immigration to Europe.

The question of African youth treading dangerous voyages at great peril to reach the shores of Europe or America will continue to engage the attention of African political leaders until the question of controlling Africa's resources under a united government is resolved.

It was Colonel Gaddafi who also emphasized:

"Man's freedom is lacking if somebody else controls what he needs, for need may result in man's enslavement of man".

In another interview, Colonel Gaddafi, campaigning to chair the African Union (AU) had this to say:

"During my term in AU, I will initiate an organized compensation claim for Africa and I will fight for a greater voice for Africa in the United Nations Security Council. If they do not want to live with us fairly, it is our planet and they can go to another planet." Unfortunately, he didn't win the election to pursue this agendum. What is certain is that the Libyan leader was less enthusiastic with Arab nationalism in favor of unity with black Africa. He strongly believed that Africa's resources should be harnessed to make the continent powerful.

What is known is that Colonel Gaddafi was brutally killed by insurgents trained by Western forces a few years after his declared intentions, no matter what the foreign media may have said.

Dear Ayesha,

In 1963, the Organization of African Unity (OAU) was formed to advance cooperation and solidarity between newly independent African countries and fight against colonialism. It is important to know that way back in 1958, Kwame Nkrumah hosted the first conference of Independent African States, then Ghana, Ethiopia, Libya, Liberia, Morocco, Sudan, Tunisia, United Arab Republic (Egypt), and played a pioneering role in the establishment of the Organization of African Unity (OAU) in 1963.

Congo's Prime Minister Patrice Lumumba had said in 1958:

"This historical conference, which puts us in contact with experienced political figures from all the African countries and from all over the world, reveals one thing to us: despite the boundaries that separate us, despite our ethnic differences, we have the same awareness, the same soul plunged day and night in anguish, the same anxious desire to

make this African continent a free and happy continent that has rid itself of unrest and of fear and of any sort of colonialist domination.

"We are particularly happy to see that this conference has set as its objective the struggle against all the internal and external factors standing in the way of the emancipation of our respective countries and the unification of Africa."

Dear Ayesha,

Sad to say, Patrice Lumumba was assassinated three years after this conference. In a letter to his wife prior to this, he had written: *"I want my children, whom I leave behind and perhaps will never see again, to be told that the future of the Congo is beautiful and that their country expects them, as it expects every Congolese, to fulfill the sacred task of rebuilding our independence, our sovereignty; for without justice there is no dignity and without independence there are no free men".*

He also wrote:

"Neither brutal assaults, nor cruel mistreatment, nor torture has ever led me to beg for mercy, for I prefer to die with my head held high, unshakable faith, and the greatest confidence in the destiny of my country rather than live in slavery and contempt for sacred principles............History will one day have its say; it will not be the history taught in the United Nations, Washington, Paris, or Brussels, ... but the history taught in the countries that have rid themselves of colonialism and its puppets. Africa will write its own history and both north and south of the Sahara it will be a history full of glory and dignity"'.

*Patrice Lumumba paid the heavy price for his
commitment to the freedom of the Congo and Africa.*

Dear Ayesha,

At the same conference in 1958, President Sekou Toure
of Guinea also said: *"This Conference of Heads of State or of
Governments will stand out as one of the affirmations of their
common destiny. One of the solemn moments when they assert
their existence and their joint and firm determination to put an
end to the reign of arbitrary colonialism, to eliminate the causes
and the illegitimate means of subordinating the people of Africa
and the material and moral wealth of Africa to alien interests and
inhuman end".*

My dear Ayesha,

In the same year, 1963, when the OAU had been formed
in Addis Ababa, Emperor Haile Selassie of Ethiopia delivered a
powerful speech at the United Nations General Assembly, part of
which said:

"...until the philosophy which holds one race superior and another inferior is finally and permanently discredited and abandoned: That until there are no longer first-class and second class citizens of any nation; That until the color of a man's skin is of no more significance than the color of his eyes; That until the basic human rights are equally guaranteed to all without regard to race... ...; Until all Africans stand and speak as free beings, equal in the eyes of all men, as they are in the eyes of Heaven; Until that day, the African continent will not know peace. We Africans will fight, if necessary, and we know that we shall win, as we are confident in the victory of good over evil..."

Haile Selassie at the UN 1963

Dear Ayesha,

I am sure you are getting the mood in the early years of the founding of the Organization of African Unity in 1963. All the leaders were prepared to maintain their independence and freedom status, but I would want you to note at the time of launching the OAU Charter, Freedom Marches were going on all over the United States of America for civil and equal rights.

The Charter of the OAU at the meeting in Addis Ababa, was based on principles including the following:

"That it is the inalienable right of all people to control their own destiny,

"that freedom, equality, justice and dignity are essential objectives for the achievement of the legitimate aspirations of the African peoples,

Dedicated to the general progress of Africa,

Desirous that all African States should henceforth unite so that the welfare and wellbeing of their peoples can be assured,

Resolved to reinforce the links between our states by establishing and strengthening common institutions".

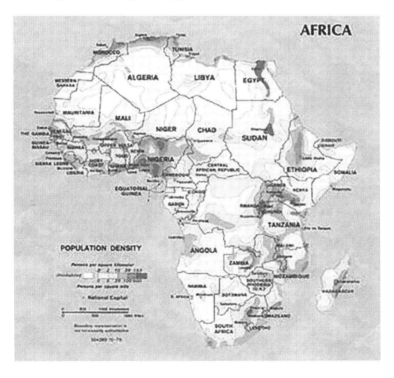

Dear Ayesha,
    What did other Founding Leaders say?

Ahmed Sekou Toure of Guinea

"At sunset when you pray to God, say over and over that each man is a brother and that all men are equal"

"Unity will not make us rich, but it can make it difficult for Africa and the African peoples to be disregarded and humiliated"
- Julius Nyerere of Tanzania

Gamel Abdel Nasser of Egypt:

"I have realized from the very beginning that our success had to depend on our complete understanding of the nature of our national history in which we had lived."

Kenneth Kaunda of Zambia:
"When you go in search
of honey you must expect to be
stung by bees."

Modibo Keita, of Mali: Development will not be possible
without peace. It is crucial that young people take on board and
embrace the notion of peace. Young people of Africa, of France
and of the diaspora, you must become the agents of peace to be
able to become the entrepreneurs of the future.

213

Modibo Keita, Kwame Nkrumah, Sekou Toure

AFRICA MUST UNITE – Kwame Nkrumah

214

Dear Ayesha,

May 2013 marked the golden jubilee of the formation of the Organization of African Unity. The leaders of African nations agreed to use the opportunity to establish a roadmap for the eventual unity and transformation of the continent, with the strong hope and belief that a global powerhouse will emerge by the year 2063. Unity, freedom, self-determination, progress and collective prosperity are the guiding objectives. The lamp posts: Pan Africanism and African Renaissance.

Following from various templates provided since the first 1963-65 meetings, African Heads of State have now initiated the Agenda 2063 which is the roadmap and masterplan for the unity of African peoples. The flagship programs and activities are expected to drive the united Africa agenda. A few of these are the following:

- Integrated High Speed Train Network
- Formulation of an African Commodities Strategy
- Establishment of the African Continental Free Trade Area
- The African Passport and Free Movement of People
- Ending all wars and civil conflicts by 2020
- Implementation of the Grand Inga Dam project to generate more energy to support power pools
- Establishment of a single African Air-transport Market
- Establishing of an annual African Economic forum
- Establishment of African Financial institutions such as African Monetary Fund, Pan-African Stock Exchange and African Investment Bank.
- Pan African E-Network
- African Outer Space Strategy
- An African Virtual and E-University
- Cyber Security
- Great African Museum to preserve and promote African heritage.

Dear Ayesha,

There is no doubt that you and your generation are now well equipped to continue the journey from Jamestown. The following quotes should guide your paths:

"It's the young trees that make the forest" – African proverb

"What you learn is what you die with" – African proverb

"Every generation must discover their own mission and fulfil it"

"Stories you read when you're at the right age never quite leave you"

"Never be limited by other people's limited imaginations" -Dr Mae Jemison, first African-American female astronaut

"Hold fast to dreams, for if dreams die, life is a broken winged bird that cannot fly". - Langston Hughes

"In recognizing the humanity of our fellow human beings, we pay ourselves the highest tribute" - Thurgood Marshall, first African American US Supreme Court member

Remember the great Bob Marley?

"Until the philosophy which holds one race superior and another inferior is finally and permanently discredited and abandoned, everywhere is war, me say war. So Much Trouble in the World".

Until my next book of Letters:
With all my Love.

Efo Kojo

LEARN TO READ:

The most important assignment I wish to leave with you after reading these letters is to read inspiring, educative and energizing books. Look for these authors, and many more I cannot list here and read all their books:

1. John Henrik Clarke – *African People in World History*
2. Cheikh Anta Diop – *Civilization or Barbarism; The Origin of African Civilization; Pre-colonial Black Africa*
3. WEB Du Bois – *The Souls of Black Folks*
4. Basil Davidson – *The African Slave Trade*
5. Ibn Battuta – *The Travels of Ibn Battuta*
6. LSB Leakey – *The Progress and Evolution of Man*
7. Robin Walker – *When We Ruled*
8. Chancellor Williams – *The Destruction of Black Civilization*
9. Tim Hashaw – *The Birth of Black America*
10. Lerone Bennett,Jr,- *Before the Mayflower*
11. Edward Baptist – *The Half Has Never Been Told*
12. Henry Louis Gates – *Stony the Road: Reconstruction, White Supremacy, and the Rise of Jim Crow*
13. 13 Kwame Nkrumah - *Africa Must Unite*
14. Martha Hanna-Smith - *Bush Medicine In Bahamian Folk Tradition*
15. Molefi Kete Asante - *The Egyptian Philosophers: Ancient African Voices From Imhotep To Akhenaten* ; *The History of Africa:The Quest for Eternal Harmony*

16. Kofi Asare Opoku - *Speak To The Winds: Proverbs from Africa*
17. David Musa - *African American Religion, A Confluent of African Traditional Religion and Christianity*
18. George G.M. James - *Stolen Legacy: The Greek Philosophy Is A Stolen Egyptian Philosophy*
19. Louis Haber - *Black Pioneers of Science and Invention*
20. William St Clair - *The Door Of No Return: The History of Cape Coast Castle and the Atlantic Slave Trade*
21. Thomas Pakenham - *The Scramble For Africa*
22. Michael A. Carson - *African- American Inventions That Changed The World:* Influential Inventors and Their *Revolutionary Creations*
23. Walter Rodney – *How Europe Underdeveloped Africa*
24. Carter G Woodson – *The Mis-education of the Negro;*
25. Shomari Wills – *Black Fortunes*
26. Vashti Harrison – *Little Leaders: Bold Women in Black History*
27. Margot Lee Shetterly – *Hidden Figures:The American Dream and the Untold Stories of the Black Women Mathematicians Who helped win the Space Race*
28. Ibram Kendi – *Stamped from the Beginning :The Definitive History of Racist Ideas in America*

AND SING:
The Redemption Song

Old Pirates, yes, they rob 1
Sold I to the merchant ships
Minutes after they took I
From the bottomless pit
But my hand was made strong
By the hand of the Almighty
We forward in this generation
Triumphantly

Won't you help to sing
These songs of freedom?
'Cause all I ever have
Redemption songs
Redemption Songs

Emancipate yourselves from mental slavery
'None but ourselves can free your minds
Have no fear for atomic energy
'Cause none of them can stop the time
How long shall they kill our prophets
While we stand aside and look? Ooh !
Some say it's just a part of it
*We've got to fulfill the **book.***